ALL OF YOUR
FEELINGS ARE
WELCOME

APPRECIATION FOR ALL OF YOUR FEELINGS ARE WELCOME

I picked up this book and, in the blink of an eye, I was halfway through. Marion's unique way of telling a story from a child's perspective, offering insights from an Aware Parenting perspective, and weaving in reparative phrases is nothing short of transformative.

But the true gold lies in the reparative phrases that Marion offers – they are like a healing balm for our old wounds of the soul. When spoken with presence, they become a profound gift to ourselves, fostering self-compassion and deeper connection.

– Maru Rojas, Aware Parenting instructor

In her beautiful new book, *All of Your Feelings are Welcome*, Marion offers a range of stories from a child's perspective, followed by clear and easy-to-read explanations from an Aware Parenting lens of what is happening behind the behaviour described in the stories, followed by loving and reparative phrases we can offer to our younger parts AND our children in those tricky parenting moments, when we often feel triggered, overwhelmed, and unsure what to say!

I love how Marion offers stories from children's perspectives – which is so often missing in other parenting books and online content. Bringing the child and their experience to the forefront really supports us to understand their perspective and why they're behaving in particular ways. It also helps us tune into our inner child and remember all the times we felt misunderstood and unsupported as a child.

I love how Marion describes the possibility of deep inner healing – when we tune into our inner child and offer those parts of ourselves the love and empathy we might have missed out on in the past, we open doors within us that can lead to more self compassion, love, grace and forgiveness. What a gift we can offer ourselves!

This book clearly describes the parallel process we undergo when we parent in this way – the more we are able to offer ourselves (and our younger parts) empathy and love, the more we can offer that to our children (and vice versa) – which is an incredibly powerful thing to realise as a parent!

## APPRECIATION FOR ALL OF YOUR FEELINGS ARE WELCOME

Thank you Marion for another beautiful book. So simple and easy to read, yet so impactful and inspiring!

– Meg Rankin, Aware Parenting instructor, Social Worker

*All of Your Feelings are Welcome* is the giant hug that every person needs, even if they didn't know they needed it.

The three sections of each chapter are the most magical, synergistic combination of different viewpoints I could ever imagine.

I didn't want to put this book down!

Marion has once again created a masterpiece that will be beloved by parents everywhere. Thank you for putting this beautiful offering into the world Marion, we are all better off for it.

– Anna Haberfield

Marion Rose's *All of Your Feelings are Welcome* is a beautifully thought-out and deeply articulated guide that gently invites you to walk in the shoes of your child self. Through her compassionate words, Marion helps you connect with that inner child, teaching you how to hold them with love and tenderness as your adult self.

This book moved me to tears countless times. Marion's ability to help you see your younger self – a child who simply needed to be seen, heard, and understood – is pure magic. She shows how, as the loving and aware adult you are now, you can finally offer that unconditional care to the child within.

This isn't just a book; it's an experience of reparenting in its most heartfelt and transformative form. A must-read for anyone on a journey of healing and self-compassion.

– Kim Cousins, Aware Parenting instructor, Registered Perinatal Nurse

Another amazing book from Marion Rose, which is really useful for whoever wants to understand children and their feelings better, and also go through the reparenting process.

What makes it unique is the first person narration that really makes you get in the child's place.

Marion very vividly describes how a child processes their feelings during various challenging situations and the shift that happens when the parent responds lovingly and compassionately to them.

She includes phrases that I would love to have heard as a child or even as an adult and that I will definitely try to embody and use for my child and for myself.

All we need is connection, and Marion has her own magic way to remind us of this.

— Eirini Anagnostopoulou, Parent Coach

I love that this book was nothing like what I expected! It was a reparenting experience on so many levels!

I expected how to's and to do's on how to heal/reparent ourselves as my conditioning has taught me that's how we learn… but then I remembered it's Marion! That not what she believes, she always trusts that I know what I need! Why would she now suddenly tell me what to do and how to do it! I love how every time she shows me there is another way (than we were taught) of thinking, doing, and living!

I love how this book is so very much Marion, filled with love and compassion and such a deep understanding for us human beings and what lies beneath our behaviour! That creates such a profound and powerful connection and safety!

I loved LOVED!!! the stories from the child's perspective! Seeing things from their perspective IS reparative! Is reparenting! It helped me trust even deeper that my kids know what they need and to lean in! To be curious and to keep connecting with myself and them! It helped me understand the process even better which helps me be patient and compassionate! And not take things personally! I felt so much hope for this beautiful connection and ease in our parenting journeys. And I felt so much willingness to welcome even more feelings, mine, my partner's and our children's.

APPRECIATION FOR ALL OF YOUR FEELINGS ARE WELCOME

I experimented with the *Inner Loving Mother/Father* phrases for myself with my kids and I could feel them hit a sweet spot. I never heard these phrases myself and I am so grateful for the inspiration!

I have read so many parenting books, including Aware Parenting books, and often felt guilt and shame afterwards. But with Marion's books I always feel such delight, hope, and love! Never have I ever read a book like Marion's. They are an experience, they are a healing in themselves! I love the clarity and simplicity with which she explains things!

It does not matter if you are new to Aware Parenting or an Aware Parenting instructor yourself, this book is a gift for everyone, no matter where in your (re)parenting journey you are!

Thank you so much Marion for inviting me to look differently, to open up my mind to endless possibilities, to reconnect with my power and to get free-er of my conditioning!

– Linde Lambrechts, Masters in Clinical Psychology, Psychotherapist, and Aware Parenting instructor

What a remarkable book this is. It is simple and yet profound at the same time. It contains everything that a parent needs in order to navigate an often challenging journey. There is a precise, distilled and concise description of Marion Rose's profound understanding of the theory of Aware Parenting. There are many stories that powerfully illustrate the experiences of children and what it is to be a human being. And all of the words of compassion and love that you have always yearned to hear, can be found in the pages of this book.

Marion shows the reader that through understanding the theory of Aware Parenting comes connection, and through connection comes the possibility to be able to resolve every parenting challenge in a way that is compassionate, effective, and kind for our children, and healing for us at the same time. Each chapter contains extraordinary clarity about the theory of Aware Parenting, eloquent descriptions from a child's perspective, and the exact phrases of compassion that parents most need to receive.

She shows us how to truly welcome our children's feelings rather than just wanting them to release or trying to listen. And she supports the reader on a journey of profound, compassionate healing for their feelings too.

Marion shares the information in a way that is most accessible. Her beautiful words will delight and inspire the reader, touching your heart and healing your soul. What a gift for parents and their children!

– Joss Goulden, Level 2 Aware Parenting instructor

Marion Rose's *All of Your Feelings are Welcome* is an extraordinary book that takes you on a deeply emotional and healing journey. Through her moving and tender words, Marion creates a safe space for readers to reconnect with the most vulnerable parts of themselves. Each chapter felt like an invitation to explore the emotions I had long buried, offering compassion and courage to meet them fully.

This book wasn't just something I read – it was something I experienced. Her stories reached parts of me I hadn't touched in years. I cried, I raged, and I sobbed as emotions I had suppressed found their way to the surface. Her words held me in a way that made me feel safe, seen, and deeply understood. It was a profoundly transformative process.

What makes this book so special is its dual purpose. It not only supports our own healing but also offers powerful tools for parenting with presence, love, and connection. The Aware Parenting insights and Inner Loving Parent phrases are deeply nourishing, providing practical guidance while also speaking directly to the heart.

This book is a gift for anyone ready to embrace healing and connection. I wholeheartedly recommend it to parents, caregivers, and anyone longing to rediscover and nurture their inner self. Marion's work is nothing short of life changing.

– Sarah Mason, Aware Parenting instructor

Published in Australia by
Loving Being Publishing
PO Box 256, Doreen, VIC 3754
marion@marionrose.net
www.marionrose.net

First published in Australia 2024
Copyright © Marion Rose 2024

All rights reserved. No part of this publication may be reproduced, stored in a retrieval system, or transmitted, in any form or by any means without the prior written permission of the publisher, nor be otherwise circulated in any form of binding or cover other than that in which it is published and without a similar condition being imposed on the subsequent purchaser.

National Library of Australia Cataloguing-in-Publication entry

 A catalogue record for this book is available from the National Library of Australia

ISBN: 978-1-7638075-0-1 (paperback)
ISBN: 978-1-7638075-1-8 (hardback)
ISBN: 978-1-7638075-2-5 (epub)

Cover layout and design by Jelena Mirkovic
Typesetting by Sophie White Design

Printed by Ingram Spark

Disclaimer: All care has been taken in the preparation of the information herein, but no responsibility can be accepted by the publisher or author for any damages resulting from the misinterpretation of this work. All contact details given in this book were current at the time of publication, but are subject to change.

The advice given in this book is based on the experience of the individuals. Professionals should be consulted for individual problems. The author and publisher shall not be responsible for any person with regard to any loss or damage caused directly or indirectly by the information in this book.

*Today, and every day, I acknowledge the Traditional Custodians of this land where I live and work, which include the Arakwal people, the Minjungbal people, the Widjabul people, and the Bundjalung people. I pay my respects to elders past, present and emerging.
I acknowledge and recognise them as the original storytellers and wisdom keepers.*

# All of Your Feelings are Welcome

Stories from a child's world to bring tears
to your eyes, healing to your inner children,
and loving presence to your parenting

MARION ROSE, PHD

*To my ancestors.*
*I'm so grateful to you that I'm here.*

# ABOUT THE AUTHOR

*I was a little girl with a lot of big feelings.*

I experienced some very significant separations, such as when I was in an incubator for the first five weeks of my life. I also had a long separation from each of my parents later on in my childhood, when my Mum lived in Australia and my Dad in England. As a result, I was often overwhelmed by feelings of sadness, fear, and powerlessness.

*The younger parts of me who longed to have their feelings heard was with me while I wrote and edited this book.*

**I've come to understand that all children have a lot of painful feelings. The more stress and trauma they experience, and the more sensitive they are, the more feelings they will need to express.**

## I believe that *all* children want to have their painful feelings heard by the significant adults in their lives.

My background is in psychology and psychotherapy. I did a degree in psychology, starting in 1987 when I was 19, because I wanted to understand myself and others more. I went on to do a PhD on postnatal depression and the mother-infant relationship at Cambridge University.

*When I started my PhD, I didn't know that this would be a profound part of healing from my own experience of being separated from my mother as a baby. I also had no idea at the time that it would be a deep foundation for my later life as a mother and an Aware Parenting instructor.*

Halfway through my PhD, despite being in weekly therapy and going to all kinds of what in those days were called 'personal development' workshops, I knew that wasn't enough for me.

So I started training as a Psychosynthesis Psychotherapist, later began my own private practice, got qualified, and did further psychotherapy training. Alongside this, I continued my academic work, becoming a Research

Fellow in infant development at Exeter University in the UK, and then a University Lecturer for MA students on The Therapeutic Relationship.

*In my twenties, my focus was on researching, training in, and understanding the effects of our infancy and childhood on us as adults. In contrast, my thirties were all about putting into practice what I'd learnt, through mothering my children and reparenting myself. I gave birth to my daughter in 2001 and my son in 2006.*

While pregnant with my daughter, I was searching for a style of parenting that would fit with all that I'd learnt in the previous 14 years in developmental psychology, pre- and peri-natal psychology, attachment theory, and psychotherapy.

As soon as I found Aware Parenting, I knew it was the paradigm I'd been looking for! It fitted with all that I had learnt, and it had a magical piece that I had never come across in all the trainings and academia, courses, and books that I'd consumed in the previous 14 years.

# The missing piece is that babies come into the world with *innate processes to heal from stress and trauma*. However, because these processes are generally not known about or recognised, parents are taught to *work against them*. These processes consist of *feeling, expressing, and releasing painful feelings.*

I became an Aware Parenting instructor in 2005, and later a Level Two instructor, and then the Regional Coordinator for Australia, New Zealand, and Indonesia.

You can find out more about Aware Parenting and its Founder, Aletha Solter, PhD, at **www.awareparenting.com**

*While working with parents, and in my own parenting, I soon realised the profound reparenting journey that we are invited to go on in parallel with parenting our children.*

As a result, I created a form of reparenting, where I combined my learnings from a number of different modalities, including: Aware Parenting, the sub-personalities and Soul work of Psychosynthesis, The Field Project, and Nonviolent Communication.

This reparenting process became a part of what I now call *The Marion Method*, which includes three core elements, Love, Will, and Conversations with Life.

The *Inner Loving Presences Practice* is a part of the Love element of *The Marion Method* and is what I include in this book.

**What I love about these practices is that they really work.**

I'm now 56, and in my own life and my 93-year-old mother's, I've seen profound and miraculous changes in each of us as well as in our relationship, since that rocky start that we had together.

I have healed from so many painful and traumatic experiences through revisiting those times, having my *Inner Loving Presences* with me, and going through the *Inner Loving Presence Process*.

**My inner dialogue has also completely changed.**

It used to be full of guilt, shame, and self-judgment, based on what I call *Disconnected Domination Culture* consciousness. Nowadays, I have a deeply self-compassionate inner dialogue, free from guilt, shame, and self-judgment. This has profoundly influenced how I feel, what I do, and how I show up in the world. My *Inner Loving Presences* are here supporting me, offering me empathy, compassion, appreciation, encouragement, and celebration.

I've also supported my Mum, who used to be full of self-judgment, shame, and guilt, to profoundly change her inner dialogue too, which has led to her having a completely different experience of life.

I've had the honour of walking beside many mentees over the years, being with their *inner children*, listening lovingly to their feelings, standing in for the soul versions of their parents and others, and supporting them in developing a deeply compassionate inner dialogue too.

I've seen these transformations happen, over and over again.

***And if I did it, I know that it is possible for people who might think it's impossible for them!***

From the scared little girl who rarely spoke, and who felt completely terrified and powerless most of the time, I'm now the mother of a 22-year-old daughter and an 18-year-old son. I'm the author of four best-selling books and the host of three podcasts, including *The Aware Parenting Podcast*, which has three million downloads (as of December 2024). I've created many tens of workshops, online courses, and other offerings about both Aware Parenting and *The Marion Method*. I've worked with many thousands of parents over the last 19 years. Many of my mentees say that their *Inner Loving Mother* has my voice. What a huge journey to take for that young woman who believed that she was 'too wounded' to become a mother.

I'm so grateful to be so deeply connected to my callings and to be sharing this work with you, as well as the younger parts of you.

Much love,
Marion
xoxox

December 2024

## AUTHOR'S NOTE

This book is an educational resource focusing on the emotional needs of children and our inner children; it is not intended to be a substitute for medical advice or treatment. Many of the behaviours and symptoms discussed can be an indication of serious emotional or physical problems in children.

Readers are advised to consult with a competent health care provider whenever children display behavioural or emotional issues, a sudden change in sleep, eating, or crying patterns, or when pain or illness are suspected. Furthermore, some of the suggested practices in this book may not be suitable under all conditions or with children suffering from certain physical or emotional challenges.

If you are ever concerned when your child is crying, or if your child's crying is suddenly high pitched, please seek advice from your health care provider. One of the reasons that children cry is when they are in physical pain, so please trust yourself if you are ever worried.

I ask that you don't do anything just because you read it in this book; rather, I invite you to always view yourself as your own authority in parenting – and to first listen in to whether what you read resonates with you, and if you do, to try it out – and observe your child's behaviour afterwards. You are the researcher and authority here.

Most of all, please listen to yourself. If you are concerned, please listen to that concern. You know your child the most. I invite you to deeply trust your perceptions and intuition.

This also applies to your own reparenting.

Please listen in to yourself as to whether to read each story. You will know if a story might be *overwhelming* for you to read, or if it's important to *not* go near a particular painful experience in your life.

*I invite you to deeply listen to your yes and your no, your willingness and not-willingness.*

Some of the beta-readers shared with me that reading the stories was incredibly powerful for them.

If you have a 'no' to reading a particular story (you might call that 'procrastination' or you might be 'shoulding' yourself or coercing yourself to read it), *please listen to that no*.

*Your body is deeply wise and knows exactly what is helpful and not helpful for you.*

If reading the stories helps you connect with big feelings, please reach out to a loving listener for support, such as an Aware Parenting instructor or Marion Method Mentor.

I trust your deep inner wisdom.

# CONTENTS

| | |
|---|---|
| About the author | 12 |
| Author's note | 16 |
| Introduction | 22 |
| About the book | 24 |
| 1. A STORY from a child's perspective | 24 |
| 2. INFORMATION from an Aware Parenting perspective | 24 |
| 3. PHRASES from Inner Loving Parents | 25 |
| Note about reading the book | 27 |

## Section 1  Expression of Feelings — 29

### 1. Crying — 30
About children and crying — 32
*Inner Loving Mother* and *Inner Loving Father* phrases — 33

### 2. Raging — 34
About children and raging — 37
*Inner Loving Mother* and *Inner Loving Father* phrases — 39

### 3. When a child is crying and raging while running away — 40
About children who are crying and running away — 42
*Inner Loving Mother* and *Inner Loving Father* phrases — 43

### 4. When a child is crying and raging while saying "Go away!" — 45
About children who are raging and saying "Go away!" — 47
*Inner Loving Mother* and *Inner Loving Father* phrases — 49

### 5. When a child is being playful before sleep — 50
About playfulness before bed — 52
*Inner Loving Mother* and *Inner Loving Father* phrases — 53

### 6. When a child isn't going to sleep — 54
About children who aren't going to sleep — 55
*Inner Loving Mother* and *Inner Loving Father* phrases — 57

## Section 2  Challenging Situations                              59

### 7.  A parent moving in to protect a child from getting hurt   60
About moving in to protect a child from being hurt               62
*Inner Loving Mother* and *Inner Loving Father* phrases          63

### 8.  Leaving the park                                          64
About play and cooperation                                       66
*Inner Loving Mother* and *Inner Loving Father* phrases          67

### 9.  When a child isn't cooperating                            68
About cooperation                                                69
*Inner Loving Mother* and *Inner Loving Father* phrases          70

### 10. When a child asks for lots of things but actually needs to cry   71
When a child asks for lots of things but really needs to cry     73
*Inner Loving Mother* and *Inner Loving Father* phrases          75

### 11. When a child is doing things that the parent asks them not to   76
When a child keeps doing something that the parent asks them not to do  79
*Inner Loving Mother* and *Inner Loving Father* phrases          80

### 12. When a child is on a screen                               81
When children are on a screen                                    82
*Inner Loving Mother* and *Inner Loving Father* phrases          83

## Section 3  Suppression of Feelings                             85

### 13. Helping a child unfreeze                                  86
Helping children with unfreezing                                 88
*Inner Loving Mother* and *Inner Loving Father* phrases          90

### 14. When a child is sucking their thumb                       91
Thumb sucking                                                    93
*Inner Loving Mother* and *Inner Loving Father* phrases          94

### 15. When a child is sucking on a dummy                        95
Sucking on a dummy                                               96
*Inner Loving Mother* and *Inner Loving Father* phrases          97

## Section 4 Aggression — 99

### 16. When a child is hitting — 100
A child who is hitting — 102
*Inner Loving Mother* and *Inner Loving Father* phrases — 103

### 17. When a child is throwing things — 105
Children who are throwing things — 107
*Inner Loving Mother* and *Inner Loving Father* phrases — 109

### 18. When a child is swearing — 110
About swearing — 112
*Inner Loving Mother* and *Inner Loving Father* phrases — 113

### 19. When a child is blaming others — 114
When children are blaming — 116
*Inner Loving Mother* and *Inner Loving Father* phrases — 117

### 20. When children are fighting — 118
About fighting — 120
*Inner Loving Mother* and *Inner Loving Father* phrases — 121

## CONCLUSION: Healing is possible — 122

## Acknowledgements — 124

## Glossary — 126
Aware Parenting Terminology — 126
Marion Method Terminology — 127

## Recommended Reading & Resources — 129
Aletha Solter's Aware Parenting Institute Website — 129
Books by Aletha Solter, PhD — 129
Books by Marion Rose, PhD — 129
Marion Rose's website — 130
Loving Presence cards by Marion Rose, PhD — 130
Aware Parenting Courses by Marion Rose, PhD — 130
Marion Method Courses by Marion Rose, PhD — 130
Podcasts by Marion Rose, PhD — 130

| | |
|---|---|
| Aware Parenting Community | 130 |
| **Ways you can work with me** | **131** |
| **If you enjoyed this book** | **132** |
| **Author Contact Page** | **133** |

# Introduction

Hello and a very big warm welcome to you!
I'm sending so much love to all the younger parts of you who might show up while you read this book.

While doing my PhD at The Winnicott Research Unit at Cambridge University, I read a book called *The Interpersonal World of the Infant: A View from Psychoanalysis and Developmental Psychology* by Daniel N. Stern. It shared stores from a baby's perspective, and it had a powerful effect on me.

When I wrote *The Emotional Life of Babies*, I loved including stories from a baby's perspective. When I was writing my next book, *I'm Here and I'm Listening*, the stories from the child's perspective also flew out of me onto the page. Unlike the rest of the book, which I edited many times, I hardly changed a word of the stories.

*I also felt deeply moved whenever I read them. I spoke one out loud to the father of my children, and he had tears in his eyes. He told me how potent it was. In fact, he said that it was one of the most powerful things he'd ever heard. I saw that it wasn't just me who was being profoundly affected by the stories.*

Once *I'm Here and I'm Listening* was published, people kept telling me that they found the stories beautifully healing for their *inner children*. Those were my favourite parts of the book. I recorded them and shared them in episodes of *The Aware Parenting Podcast*.

One day, soon after *I'm Here and I'm Listening* was published, I received a really clear calling to write a small book, full of these stories from a child's perspective. I had such a big YES to doing it. In a flash, I knew that this book wanted to come into the world after *Sound Sleep and Secure Attachment with Aware Parenting*, which is the third in my trilogy of Aware Parenting books (and which also includes stories from a baby's, child's, and teen's perspective).

Straight away I knew that (*unlike* my Aware Parenting trilogy of books!) this would be a relatively small book. I could imagine it being on bedside tables. I pictured people reading the stories and being touched to tears; experiencing deep healing for their inner children.

I also knew that the book wouldn't just include the stories. It was clear to me that each story would be followed by some information from an Aware Parenting perspective, and some Inner Loving Presence phrases (from *The Marion Method*).

The book came through me so quickly. I wrote it in several writing sessions over about two and a half weeks. This is the exact book right here, with edits!

**So here it is, a book to reach the parts of you that other books might not reach.**

**A book to touch your heart and speak to the younger parts of you.**

**A book to support deep and transformative healing.**

*I'm so willing for you* to feel a deep sense of healing, repair, and unconditional love for your *inner children* as a result of reading this book.

And if you're a parent, I'm so willing for this book to also help you feel more compassionate towards your child/ren, and even clearer about how to respond to them in ways that align with Aware Parenting.

## About the book

There are three elements to each chapter:

1. **A *STORY* from a child's perspective** (illustrating children's feelings and adults' responses from an Aware Parenting lens);

2. **INFORMATION from an Aware Parenting perspective** (including information about which Aware Parenting books you might like to read if you want to learn more);

3. **PHRASES from *Inner Loving Parents*** (from *The Marion Method*).

Each of these elements has *two* purposes. One is for our *inner children*, and one is for those of you who are parents.

I'd love to outline them for you, to support you in receiving the full benefits of this book.

### 1. A *STORY* from a child's perspective

The *first* purpose is for your *inner children* to have deeply healing and reparative experiences when you imagine being the child in the story.

The *second* is for *parents*: to receive ideas about how you might most helpfully respond during similar moments in your parenting.

### 2. *INFORMATION* from an Aware Parenting perspective

The *first* purpose is to help you understand your *inner children* more, both in terms of what you felt and experienced in your childhood, and what you might have needed back when you were a child.

The *second* is for *parents*: to understand more of the theory of Aware Parenting in each particular topic.

### 3. *PHRASES* from Inner Loving Parents

**The *first* purpose is for you to hear the relevant *inner loving phrases*, to support healing for the *younger parts* of you.**

Connecting with our *Inner Loving Parents* is a core part of the *The Marion Method*. Our *Inner Loving Mother* and *Inner Loving Father* are *not based* on our *actual* parents. Instead, they are like the *archetypes* of what *we would most love to experience and hear* (or loved to have heard as children) from our parents.

**There are many different ways to connect with our *Inner Loving Parents*. I invite you to start with one parent, whether it is your *Inner Loving Mother* or *Inner Loving Father*.**

Some people enjoy imagining their physical presence, such as sitting beside us, holding our hand, putting their hand on our back, or giving us a hug. Others enjoy a visual presence, such as an image. Others simply 'hear' the words. Or you might experience a combination of these, or something completely different. Each of us is unique and we will all have different ways of engaging in this practice.

*I invite you to feel in to which of the phrases, if any, resonate with you.*

The practice starts with reading the phrases, and imagining that you are hearing those words from your *Inner Loving Mother* or *Inner Loving Father*. Alternatively, you might write them down, speak them out loud, or ask a friend, *empathy buddy*[1], Aware Parenting instructor[2], or *Marion Method Mentor*[3] to read them to you.

**Actually hearing these words from someone else is often an important part of the process, which is why I recommend having the support of at least one person who repeatedly offers us loving compassion. This**

---

1　An *empathy buddy* is someone we regularly connect with, with whom we give and receive empathy. This is where we listen lovingly to each other, without giving advice, suggestions, or judgment. This can be in person, over the phone, by video call, by voice message, or by text. This term came from Nonviolent Communication.

2　You can find Aware Parenting instructors in Australia, New Zealand, and Indonesia on my website: www.marionrose.net, and in the rest of the world at www.awareparenting.com

3　You can find *Marion Method Mentors* on my website, at www.marionrose.net

*is because we are replicating the process that would have happened to us as children, where we internalised how we were responded to. This time, we are internalising unconditional love and support, free from* **Disconnected Domination Culture** *conditioning.*

Another important thing to know is that whatever your response to those words, expressing your reaction to them is an essential part of the healing process. So, although you might feel touched, moved, or relieved, you might also feel disbelief, frustration, or other uncomfortable feelings.

I invite you to welcome whatever your response is. *The healing happens when we feel and express whatever shows up in response to the love that we receive from our Inner Loving Parents.* That might be tears, or warmth, or outrage, or something else.

***It's really important that whatever you feel and think in response to the loving phrases is expressed and lovingly heard.***

You might write your responses down, and keep responding to those from the perspective of your *Inner Loving Parent*, or you might ask your *empathy buddy*, Aware Parenting instructor, or *Marion Method Mentor* to respond with unconditionally loving phrases to whatever shows up for you.

*Please listen in to yourself and whether you need to reach out for some listening support with those feelings.*

**The *second* purpose is for parents. As we increasingly *internalise* the loving phrases, similar and relevant phrases then also come more *naturally* to us when we speak to our child/ren.**

Offering our children loving compassion, whatever they are feeling and however they are behaving, is a central part of Aware Parenting. The more we receive loving phrases and know from first-hand experience how enjoyable it is to receive them, the more we are likely to want to express them to our child/ren. Doing so will also increasingly become second nature to us as we keep practicing those responses.

ALL OF YOUR FEELINGS ARE WELCOME

## Note about reading the book

I invite you to trust what you feel called to read. Perhaps you'll scan through the contents and read chapters that seem relevant for you. Or maybe you'll just open a page at random and start reading there.

*I invite you to deeply listen in to, and trust, your yeses and noes. I trust that you know which stories you are ready and willing to read, and whether there are any that are important for you to NOT read at the moment.*

I wonder what you're wanting from this book, and why you felt called to read it now?

**Whatever it is that you want, I'm so willing for you to experience that, as well as tender compassion, gentle healing, and deep empowerment.**


So much love to you,
Marion

December 2024

I'm sending love to here and now you,
and to all the younger parts of you.

# SECTION 1

# Expression of Feelings

## CHAPTER ONE

# Crying

*Mummy, my eyes feel a funny feeling around the edges, and it's like I've got a lump in my throat. You're talking to me, but it's really important that I don't look in your eyes. I don't even know why that is, but I'm trying to make sure our eyes don't meet. You're talking, but I can't even really hear you, because my heart is racing and the blood is rushing through my ears like a noisy jet plane.*

*My body is like a factory, with machines everywhere making noises, moving lots, doing busy things. I don't know what to do. I start to walk away from you. I don't know what's going on. I feel so alone with all of this. You don't even seem to notice. You're just talking on at me about the same old things. Can't you see I'm drowning in the machine noise in here? My heartbeat is getting louder and louder. You're on a different planet to me. It's as if I don't exist. I'm floating away, so I can hardly hear you any more.*

*But what's this?*

*You walk towards me, and you gently turn your head to the side, close to mine.*

*I look up, and I see you. I see your eyes, and I see the love in them.*

*I see you seeing me.*

*Immediately, the full feelings in my eyelids transform into tears. The red and raw become the blue and flowing. The tears start to roll down my cheeks. You slowly and tentatively reach your arm out, to my shoulder. I know that you're asking me if I am willing to be touched. I nod, a tiny amount, but you see it, you see me, and your arm lands. Contact is*

*Chapter one: Crying*

*made. The stream becomes a waterfall. The tears become sobs. My chest heaves, pushing out the feelings I've been holding in for days. The sobs change again, this time into wailing.*

*I'm so glad you're here with me, Mum, because for a moment I feel scared. A thought – "Is there something wrong with me?" comes into my mind, and as I look at you, you see that thought, somehow – are you a magician, Mum? – You see me thinking that and you gently smile and speak, "There's nothing wrong with you, sweetheart. Your tears are normal and beautiful. I welcome them all. I'm here with you."*

*I fall into your arms, a rag doll of hurt and pain, and your arms fold across my shoulders and my back. I can feel your warmth. Oh, I can feel! I feel SO much, Mum. My heart is hurting so much. And there's nothing stopping these feelings now. I thought I needed to hold them in. I thought you wouldn't love me if I showed them to you. But you DO love me, Mum. You DO love me! You aren't leaving me.*

*But Mum, you DID leave me. You left me alone. I didn't want you to leave me. I felt so sad. I feel it now, a sadness that is like a bottomless ocean. I cry and I cry and I cry. YOU DID LEAVE ME! WHY did you leave me, Mum? Didn't you love me? Didn't you want me? Did I do something wrong? I thought you were never going to come back again. I cry and wail and sob, and you hold me. Your soft words of love, telling me that you're here with me now, help me feel safe to let it all out. The ocean of hurt is still here. But it's emptying. Maybe it isn't bottomless, after all.*

*You hold me, but you don't rock me like you used to do. It was strange, but when you used to do that when I was a little kid, I didn't actually feel more relaxed. I kind of felt agitated. I stopped crying, but I felt kind of weird. I'm so glad that you're not doing that this time. You're still and warm. Your heart beating is the only movement I can feel from you. But I'm making lots of big movements while I cry. My mouth opens wide as I wail. Tears still stream down my face. There's snot from my nose pooling on your t-shirt.*

*The sobbing settles. The ocean seems much smaller now, a gentle sea, not the big deep one it was before. We're on a little boat together, bobbing on the surface. My breath changes, I sigh, and a wind skitters past. I feel so much lighter and freer. You're here with me. You whisper, "I welcome all of your tears. I hear how sad you were when I went away. I'm always here to listen to your feelings about it."*

*The factory noise has gone, and instead there's wind through the trees coming through the window, and a bird sings. I ask you if we can look at photos from that time when you went away, and you smile with a big yes. I feel calm in my heart, ready to see them with you.*

*I love you, Mum.*

*I love you.*

## About children and crying

Children naturally heal from stressful and traumatic experiences through crying with the loving support of an adult. To heal, they need to know that they are physically and emotionally safe in the present moment, so they can revisit the past experiences, and feel and express the feelings from then. Crying helps them release emotions such as sadness and grief which were experienced in times of loss and separation, as well as times when their needs weren't met, or when they were overwhelmed. When we are lovingly present with a crying child (or our *inner child*), they can release those feelings in healing ways and become deeply relaxed and present. Afterwards, we might notice that they are loving towards us, other children, and animals. They might sleep more restfully that night. They might be more willing to cooperate, and find it easier to concentrate and think clearly.

If you want to learn more about crying, I invite you to read *Tears and Tantrums* by Aletha Solter, PhD. and my book, *I'm Here and I'm Listening*.

## *Inner Loving Mother* and *Inner Loving Father* phrases

I love you when you're crying.

I love you when you're sad.

I will always be here to listen to your tears.

There's nothing wrong with you when you cry, sweetheart.

Your tears are natural and healing.

I'm here with you.

I'll stay right here with you.

I won't ever leave you alone when you're crying.

I will always come to you when you need me.

Your crying is never too much for me.

You are never too much for me.

Your feelings are not too big for me.

I can be with all of your feelings.

I will always be with you when you're feeling upset.

I'm sending love to all the times you were left alone.

I welcome your sadness.

I love you, however you feel.

## CHAPTER TWO

# Raging

*I let myself in the door and I start walking to my bedroom. What a shocking day at school that was. You walk out of the kitchen with a smile, Dad, and immediately, my defences are up. I hardly hear what you're saying, some stupid nice rubbish about how my day was. You don't really care. You don't really want to know how it was for me. I know, because any time I try to tell you, you just deflect, and I've had it with pretending. I just want you to leave me alone, so I can go to my room and listen to music.*

*You walk towards me along the hallway, and through the fog of my frustration, I see your eyes, questioning, searching for mine. But I don't want you to see me. Not if it means yet again you trying to get me to "see sense", trying to calm me down, trying to make me wrong for feeling what I feel. That sucks.*

*But what's this, Dad? Something's different.*

*You don't have that judgy look on your forehead. I see warmth in your eyes. Something shifts inside me. A block of concrete falls, collapses. The ground moves. "WHAT?" I say to you.*

*More warmth, no judgment. What the hell is going on, Dad? This is different.*

*More concrete breaks inside me. I can almost feel the dust rising. "WHAT DO YOU WANT, DAD?" I shout. From underneath the concrete comes an ancient creature, old and powerful. Is it a dinosaur? A dragon? I don't know and I don't care, but I can feel it, stretching arms, big claws, fangs, huge long legs, and talons. A roar comes out of me.*

*"I hate you, Dad. You just DON'T GET IT."* And I know what happens next. It always does. You get angry. You punish me. You judge me. You send me to my room. I hunch, ready for it.

*But it doesn't come. I'm momentarily curious.*

*I look up.*

*You tell me that you hear that I hate you.*

*You say that you understand how painful it is for me when you don't get me.*

*You nod, with understanding and that stupid warmth in your eyes.*

*We're off the map now, Dad. I don't know what happens here.*

*More concrete breaks off. My world is tumbling apart. The creature stands up bigger, stronger.*

*"I HATE YOU. YOU NEVER LISTEN TO ME."*

*That'll do it. You've never stayed before. You can't take it.*

*Hang on. But you're still here. What's going on?*

*Right, the rage erupts. "RAAAAAAAHHHHHHHH" I roar. But you don't judge me. You stand there, warm and strong and there.*

*That's it. I'm a goner. It's all coming out now. I stomp around. "I AM SO FED UP WITH THIS. I hate you. I hate school. It's such a bunch of crap. I hate Mr. Reed. He treats me like I'm an idiot. I HATE sitting at that stupid desk all day. And the stuff that's happening at lunchtime, I have HAD ENOUGH OF IT ALL. Why do you make me go there every day. It's TORTURE. WHY, DAD? WHY? I HATE YOU."*

*There's still a bit of me that thinks you're going to start lecturing me now, but clearly, that Dad isn't here, because you're still here with me, still listening. Still a strong rock for me. Your eyes still searching for mine, you nod, letting me know that you understand.*

*That breaks me. Another bit of concrete falls. "I AM SOOOOOO ANGRY. I HATE IT SO MUCH." I am a prehistoric creature. My rage fills the world. I am more powerful than anything. More powerful than Mr. Reed, more powerful than the kids who laugh at me, more powerful than my little brother poking fun at me. "I AM SOOOOOO ANGRY."*

*You hear me. You hear me, Dad. I can hardly believe it.*

*I'm this huge strong prehistoric creature, but you are bigger than me and stronger than me, and I'm safe, even though this rage is SO huge. I start angry crying, and you are there.*

*I look in your eyes and the wildness in me roars like a wounded animal. I see you meet me there. My feelings are so big, but their bigness doesn't overpower you. You meet me in it. I am safe.*

*Wow, I am safe, Dad.*

*I roar and roar some more, and I remember all those times you told me to "be quiet" and to "calm down" and to "stop playing that stupid game" that I actually really loved, and I roar towards you too. How DARE you speak to me like that, Dad. You are supposed to be my Dad. You're supposed to listen to me, and love me. "I HATE YOU!" I say once more. And you take it, Dad. You don't get angry. You don't leave me. You don't react. You're here with me. I can see you, Dad. I can feel you. I'm safe with you now.*

*I'm not sure about this, because I haven't cried with you since I was a little kid, and I remember that very last time, when you told me to "grow up". But I think that perhaps this new you won't do that.*

*Underneath the raging dinosaur is a little rain-drenched sad puppy, just wanting to be loved. I stop raging, and I fall into your big arms. I'm still a bit unsure, but Dad, you come through for me. I start to cry, big sobs burst out of me, and you hold me, Dad. I've been wanting this for so long. You're really there for me. You really love me. The concrete dam has broken and the old murky water pours out of me. You're there. You keep on being there. You love this heartbroken me. Tears fall down and down and down. There are so many tears in here, Dad. I needed to hold them all in.*

*I didn't like being judged and shamed when I cried. I'm letting the tears out now, and you love me. YOU LOVE ME, DAD! Wow! I can feel more concrete breaking, as I sob in your big warm arms. We're here together, at the centre of the world, and you love me. I sigh, and sigh again.*

*The tears come to an end. I look up, a bit unsure, but you look down at me, and smile. "I love you," you say, and now I know that you do, Dad, you really do. I sigh, and smile, and cuddle back into you.*

*"Can I tell you about what happened at school today, Dad?" I ask, and you nod, that smile still on your face. And I launch into the story, knowing that you're really listening this time....*

## About children and raging

Raging and tantrums are one of the key ways that children move out of the fight, flight, or freeze response and return to a state of calm relaxation. However, for that to happen, they need to have two important elements in place.

Firstly, they need to have the presence of an adult who helps them know that they are physically and emotionally safe. Secondly, they need to be able to revisit the past, where the painful or traumatic experience originally happened.

In Aware Parenting, this is called the *'balance of attention'*, and it's the exact point where there's enough safety in the present so they can feel the painful feelings from the past.

This *balance of attention* is vital, because if they believe they're not safe, they will need to stay in fight, flight, or freeze. Only when they really know that they are now safe can they descend out of those survival responses into the vulnerability of releasing the energy mobilised to survive.

*A child who is hitting, pushing, or kicking is still in fight mode. A child who is unmoving and numb is in freeze.*

Children's angry rages are healthy forms of release if they are accompanied by crying (or soon give way to crying). Body movements while crying can help release the energy that was mobilised for fight or flight.

## When children feel safe, their movements during angry crying are *not* aggression targeted against another person. If children hit, kick, or push, they are still in fight mode.

During a healthy rage release, movements while crying might include feet stomping and arm movements, jumping up and down, or (in younger children) falling to the floor and flailing around.

Once children have been raging and *angry crying* for a while – where they are making lots of vigorous movements and may be screaming – they will often move to *sad crying*. It's here where they will often want to be held by us, if that wasn't the case before.

The *angry crying* may be releasing feelings of powerlessness, frustration, anger, or rage, and the *sad crying* might be expressing emotions such as sadness, hurt, disappointment, or overwhelm.

If they have someone to be with them all the way through the process, so they can express the whole chunk of feelings, they will generally come out the other side, feeling a deep sense of relaxation in their muscles. They will often look clearer, make relaxed eye contact, smile, express love, be more gentle with others, and sleep more peacefully.

However, if they don't get to complete a whole cycle and don't express the whole chunk of feelings, those feelings might bubble out later on that day or in the middle of the night, to be released then.

If you want to learn more about raging, I invite you to read *Tears and Tantrums* by Aletha Solter, PhD, and my book, *I'm Here and I'm Listening*.

### *Inner Loving Mother* and *Inner Loving Father* phrases

I won't leave you alone when you're angry.

I love you when you feel and express your rage.

Your anger won't hurt me.

I'm here to keep us both safe.

I am so comfortable with all of your big feelings.

You and your anger are safe with me.

I will stay here with you while you're raging.

I will stay with you for as long as you need me.

I'm here and I'm listening.

Your rage is beautiful.

Your rage is your power.

You are so powerful.

I love your power.

I see how powerful you are.

I love every single part of you.

I love you when you're angry.

I will always stay with you when you're raging.

There's nothing you can do that would send me away from you.

I love you unconditionally.

I love you and all of your feelings.

CHAPTER THREE

# When a child is crying and raging while running away

*I sit looking out of the window, a tear falling down my cheek. I see you coming towards me, Mum, and I look away, and see my reflection in the window. You bend down and ask me how I am, and the feelings in my chest and throat and eyes get bigger. Are you making them happen? I don't like them. I don't like it.*

*I get up, and run out the back door, as tears start falling down my cheeks. I need to get away from you. When I can't see you, I feel nothing again. The tears stop. I gaze at the grass and the ground, not really seeing them.*

*It's like I'm not really here. I'm not really anywhere.*

*I hear the back door bang, and you're here again. Immediately, I can feel again. Tears jump into my eyes. This is some kind of weird magic, Mum. How do you make me feel? I stumble up, and start to run away again. When I can't feel you, I can't feel me, and I don't want to feel those ouchy feelings right now.*

*But then there's nothing again. Usually you leave me alone at this point. It's happened so many times now. You tell me to come back if I have feelings to tell you, but I never do. I don't want to feel. It hurts too much. And I can't feel without you, anyway. You do that wizardy magic stuff and I only feel when I'm with you.*

*You turn around to go inside. I see you out of the corner of my eye. The feelings start to go. But then you turn back again, and start walking towards me. What on earth is going on? This never happens. And it's weird, cos the closer you come to me, the more I can feel these feelings again, and I don't like them. I don't WANT to feel them. WHY are you doing this? Why don't you just leave me alone like you usually do?*

*I start to run to the end of the garden. "Leave me alone!" I shout. That usually works. You usually go away, and then I feel nothing again. But there really is something different happening this time, Mum, because you don't go away. I can see from your face that you heard what I said, and I can see you taking it in, and slowing down, but you keep moving towards me.*

*You call out, "I hear that you want me to leave you alone, sweetheart, but I'm not willing to leave you alone when you're upset, because I'm here to help you feel safe with your feelings. And I'm here and I'm listening." What on earth is this? Straight away there's a kind of drop in my body, and tears start falling out of my eyes. I'm crying. Where did that come from? I didn't even know I was upset.*

*I cry louder and louder, and run faster and faster, to get to the bottom of the garden, under the hedge, where I often go to hide. You're not running, but you keep walking towards me, and the closer you get, the more I sob. I feel so much, Mummy. I sit under the hedge and you come close to me, but still a little way away. I'm full on sobbing now. "I'm here with you, sweetheart," you say, "I'm listening. I see how upset you are. I'm right here with you."*

*I kind of want to be alone but I also want you to come closer. I'm right in these feelings and although it's really painful, somehow it's not as bad now you're here with me and I know that you won't leave me alone. You put your hand out and gently touch my knee. I cry more. There's tears and there's snot and it's all over the place but I put my head on your hand and I cry so hard that I think I'm crying out all the sea in my tears. I'm crying forever and ever. I'm crying with you. I look up, and I see that now I'm halfway on your lap. You don't say much, just, "I'm listening," once in a while, while I cry all the tears of the world.*

*It's even more weird, Mum, because there don't seem to be many more tears left. I was scared to feel them, but I did feel them, and I actually feel much lighter and even a tiny bit happy. I didn't think that would happen!*

*All that time I've been running away from you and running away from those tears and I actually feel really relieved now. I can even look you in the eye. "I had the most horrible day today Mum," I say, and you nod, and invite me to share more, so I tell you all about it.*

*Phew, that was a lot to let out. We walk hand in hand back up the garden, and our dog Bobby comes out for cuddles. I can feel my body now. I can feel my hand and Bobby's fur.*

*I'm back.*

*I'm here now.*

*I'm here now with you. And you're here with me.*

## About children who are crying and running away

When children have big feelings that need to be expressed, they need to know that they are physically and emotionally safe in order for the crying to be healing.

The *balance of attention* is created when they feel safe in the present moment – through our presence and connection – while also staying connected with the feelings from the past.

If they are running away from us when they are crying, there can be two main reasons for that.

The *first* is that they are in the flight part of the fight or flight response. They are literally fleeing and are also trying to flee from their painful emotions.

The *second* is if when they tried to cry in the past, they were shushed, distracted, ignored, or punished. Thus, they are running away when they need to cry because they have learned that the adults around them are not comfortable with their crying. They prefer to be alone rather than experience distraction, judgment, or anger from an adult. As a result, they don't feel the safety they need to feel and express the painful feelings, and will dissociate instead. In other paradigms, sometimes this behaviour is referred to as 'sulking'.

***With both of these causes, they need our loving presence to know that they are safe now to cry with us.***

When they run far enough away from us, they may stop crying, but it's likely that they have dissociated from those feelings and the accompanying tears. When they feel more of our presence, they feel connected again with their feelings and the healing process can continue. When they complete the whole cycle of crying and release the complete chunk of feelings, they will come out the other side, into a calm state of homeostasis.

If you want to learn more about the physiology of feelings, the fight, flight, or freeze response, and healing from stress and trauma, I invite you to read *Healing Your Traumatized Child* by Aletha Solter, PhD, and my book, *I'm Here and I'm Listening*.

## *Inner Loving Mother* and *Inner Loving Father* phrases

I see that you're running away, sweetheart.

I see that you want to get away from the pain and the hurt.

Of course you do, my darling. It's so painful, isn't it?

I'm so sorry for all the times I wasn't here to listen to your feelings when you were upset.

I'm here to listen to all of those feelings.

I'm here to listen to anything you want to say to me.

I will stay with you, whatever you say.

I will be with your feelings, however you feel.

I will stay close with you, for as long as you need to cry.

I understand how much pain you're in right now.

I'm listening.

ALL OF YOUR FEELINGS ARE WELCOME

I'm here to listen.

I'm here to help you know that you're safe with me now.

I acknowledge all the times that I haven't protected you from being hurt, and all the times I've done things that have been painful for you.

I take responsibility for all the times I've said or done things that have been painful for you.

And I'm here to listen to all the feelings you have about that.

I love you.

CHAPTER FOUR

# When a child is crying and raging while saying "Go away!"

*I storm into my bedroom. I HATED today. I throw my school bag on the floor. I actually cannot believe how terrible today was. I don't even know what to do with myself after all of what happened.*

*And then I hear your voice, Dad, and you're clearly coming to find me. You poke your head around my door.*

*"How was it, today?" you ask.*

*I open my bag and start dumping things out of it.*

*"You okay?" you say.*

*"LEAVE ME ALONE!" I shout.*

*I see the surprise in your eyes, and you leave. Ha! It always works.*

*But you know, Dad, sometimes I wish you'd actually stay with me.*

*Yeah, but that will never happen!*

*But then there's some kind of miracle. I wonder if you read my mind. You come back.*

*"Rough day?" you say.*

*"Didn't I tell you to GO AWAY??" I shout, feeling it all now.*

*That'll do it.*

*But you stay. I look up. I take a glance at your face.*

*You nod your head, as if you understand.*

*"I hear that you want me to go away, love, but I'm not willing to leave you alone when you're upset, because I don't think that's the most helpful thing for you. I'm here and I'm listening."*

*"I HATE YOU!" I rage. "YOU NEVER LISTEN TO ME!"*

*You stand there, nodding, while my eyes point daggers at you.*

*"AAAAARRRRGGHHHHHHHHH!" I bare my teeth at you.*

*You stay. You're still there. And wow, Dad, you're still calm. I don't believe it. You've never stayed with me before when I feel this way. You're there, and you're not leaving me this time.*

*"I AM SOOOO MAD RIGHT NOW!" I glare at you.*

*You stay.*

*Oh Dad, something funny is happening. Something's collapsing in me. Out come the words, "I feel SOOOO angry!"*

*"I hear you. I'm here with you," you say.*

*It's so weird, because then I feel even more angry.*

*"Shut up, stupid Dad. You are SO stupid!" I rage back.*

*"I'm right here with you, love. I'm not going to leave you alone with these feelings this time. I'm staying right here with you."*

*You're a big massive tree, and I feel you and your big strong roots in the ground. You don't waver, you don't fall. I'm finally safe with you. I'm safe. Oh Dad, I'm safe with you!*

*I start to sob. This hasn't ever happened before. I cry with you, Dad, and you STILL don't leave me. I cry some angry tears with you, until all the anger has come out of me.*

*You open your arms, and I fall in them, sobbing and sobbing. It hurts SO much, Dad. My heart hurts. My eyes hurt. I hurt. I've been hurting forever. I'll be hurting forever.*

*"I'm here with you. I'm listening," you gently say.*

*My heart hurts so much. But I also feel this kind of sweetness, like maple syrup on my pancakes. I feel so much pain, but here in your arms, it's different.*

*I cry and cry and cry. I've been longing for this forever and I didn't even know it. You stay and you stay and you stay. I didn't think that you loved me, Dad, but now I know that you do. You really do.*

*I'm still crying, but it's gentle crying now. My heart doesn't hurt any more. My throat's a bit sore, though, from that raging I did. I sigh, and shudder, and a last few tears come out.*

*I didn't ever think there was going to be an end to the pain, Dad, but there is. I feel it. I can feel your chest and your arms and I feel safe and warm.*

*Now I can feel my heart, but it's love I feel, not pain. Wow. You love me and I love you. And you keep on holding me, as if we've been here forever. I start to quietly tell you about what happened, and you listen, and you nod, and you hear me.*

*I feel so relieved.*

*I feel so different.*

*I feel so free.*

## About children who are raging and saying "Go away!"

When children are feeling rage, they need the presence of an adult for the raging to be healing. When they feel physically and emotionally safe, they can move out of the fight/flight response into the resolution of that response, releasing the tension, stress and accumulated feelings, so they can feel calm and relaxed again.

Of course we want to honour a child's no and their needs for agency and choice, which is why it's so vital to *observe* our child. If we do go away, do they become *calm,* or do they *dissociate*? With Aware Parenting, we can tell the difference. Gently experimenting with the amount of closeness and the loving words we offer, we can find a way to help them feel *safe* enough to express those feelings.

When we stay, they might start raging more loudly. It's always important for us to observe closely here. Does it seem as though our closeness is helping them feel more physical and emotional safety to express the big feelings they've been holding inside? It's only through deep observation and inner listening that we can be sure about what's really going on and what they need.

When we can support them to feel safe, their aggressive behaviour will stop, and they will move into angry crying. If we continue to stay present, this angry crying will often give way to deep sobbing, as they release terror, grief, or overwhelm. They may continue to cry loudly for some time.

We might find that we're offering the same physical presence, and they've moved from a sense of pushing up against our presence, to sinking into it. That can give us reassurance that our support was helpful, and continues to be so. If we can stay present right to the end of the feelings, we're likely to find that their muscles become deeply relaxed and they make soft eye contact. We are likely to notice that the painful feelings have left their body and they feel connected again.

If you want to learn more about raging and tantrums, I invite you to read *Tears and Tantrums* by Aletha Solter, PhD, and my book, *I'm Here and I'm Listening*.

Chapter Four: When a child is crying and raging while saying "Go away!"

### ***Inner Loving Mother* and *Inner Loving Father* phrases**

I hear that you want me to go away.

And I'm not willing to leave you alone with these big feelings.

It's my responsibility to stay with you when you feel big feelings.

I won't leave you alone with this, sweetheart.

I'm not scared of your big feelings.

You are not too much for me.

Your feelings are not too much for me.

I'm here to keep you safe while you express these feelings.

I'm here with you.

I love you when you're angry.

I love you when you're raging.

There's nothing you could say or do that would stop me from loving you.

I'm going to keep staying here with you while you rage.

I won't leave you alone with this, sweetheart.

I'm staying here.

I will always be here when you need me.

My love for you is bigger than the world.

I love you unconditionally.

I love you, however you feel.

CHAPTER FIVE

# When a child is being playful before sleep

*I know it's past bedtime, Mum, but I'm so wired that I just can't sleep. I'm like a bouncy bunny, cos all I want to do is jump around.*

*I know you want me to calm down and be serious, but this smile comes out and I just want to be silly and funny. I start pretending to fall over. I stick out my tongue. I sing loudly. I run from my toys to my teddy to my books. I'm wild, I'm silly, I'm moving. I can't stop moving. I'm here, and now I'm here, and now, over here, look! Look, Mum! I can climb on to the table! I can hide behind the curtains. You'll never catch me! I'm a big bunny!*

*I feel fun but I feel scared. I know you don't like me being like this. You get that really serious look on your face. Your forehead gets all wrinkly and your mouth goes into a line and I tense up, ready for you to tell me to calm down. Ugh. I HATE trying to calm down. I try to turn myself into a pretzel to calm down, but I just feel all tense, like I'm about to burst.*

*But what's this, Mum?*

*You come out of the kitchen and you've got the oven mitts on your hands and Dad's apron around your shoulders. You're wearing the googly glasses that I got for my birthday. What is going on?*

*"Where is my lovely darling bunny?" you shout in a silly voice.*

*Me? Are you talking about me? You bump into the wall and look surprised. "Where ARE you?" you say.*

Chapter Five: When a child is being playful before sleep

*Well, I have no idea what's going on, but I think you want me to join in! I jump up in the air with a big smile!*

*"Oh THERE you are!" you say, and come towards me, but then you seem to trip up just before you get to me, and you land on the floor. Where has my serious Mum gone and who are you?*

*"Whatever you do, you're not going to run around the house, are you, bunny?" you say. Oh, I get this, you actually WANT me to carry on being silly. Wow! I feel all this joy bubbling out of me! You love me! You accept me! You want me to keep being a bouncy bunny!*

*I become the biggest, bounciest bunny in the world! I jump so high each time that I nearly touch the ceiling! BOING! BOING! BOING!*

*Now, you really are different, because you're bouncing around after me! We BOUNCE on the sofa, we BOUNCE on the beds, we BOUNCE all around the house. And I'm laughing so hard, Mum. I don't think I've ever laughed so much with you. And you're laughing too. I LOVE THIS SO MUCH! Can we bounce and bounce and bounce all night? We bounce into each other, and each time, you give me a big hug. I can see your warm smile. I can see your love.*

*Something strange is happening, because the more we bounce and laugh and I see your warm smile, the bounce is going out of me. My bounce battery is running out.*

*You know what, Mum, I actually feel quite tired. I start to bounce towards my bed, and you follow me, pretending to nibble on carrots and grass as we go. "How's my little bunny?" you ask. I tell you how tired I'm feeling, and we gently bounce into bed.*

*You lie next to me, and I don't feel bouncy any more. My body feels all full and slow. I'm like a slow sloth. I cuddle up with you. "I liked being bouncing bunnies with you, Mummy."*

*I close my sloth eyes, feeling your heart beating next to mine.*

*I wonder if I'll dream of carrots.*

## About playfulness before bed

*Children have natural inbuilt relaxation responses that are meant to help them fall asleep when they're sleepy. The main ways those responses work are through laughing and playing, or crying and raging with our loving support. As they get older, sharing their feelings through talking increasingly joins these relaxation-through-release responses.*

Rather than trying to get them to 'calm down' when they are playful, if we cooperate with their playfulness, they can feel deeply connected and relaxed, by releasing uncomfortable feelings through the play and laughter.

In Aware Parenting, there is a particular form of play called *attachment play*, described in detail in the book of the same name by Aletha Solter, PhD. There are nine different types of *attachment play*, and some of those support our children's healing through laughter.

Power-reversal games are one of the nine types of *attachment play*. In power-reversal games we take the less powerful role, and pretend to be scared, surprised, or angry. This can help children release feelings of powerlessness, so they can then feel powerful. Another type of game is nonsense play, where we act silly and goofy; this can help them release feelings related to competence. There are many other opportunities to support our children to process their feelings through *attachment play*.

When we deeply trust that our child wants to sleep, knows how to feel relaxed, and needs our help to release these feelings, we are more likely to be willing to join in and cooperate with their natural relaxation response.

*Sometimes the laughter and play will bring enough connection and release for them to feel relaxed enough to sleep.*

*But at other times, they will have deeper and more painful feelings that are preventing them from being able to feel relaxed enough to fall asleep, even if they are really tired. The play can help those feelings bubble to the surface.*

In this case, the play and laughter might turn into crying or raging, which is another form of their relaxation-through-release response. When we can listen lovingly to those feelings, they can let them out, and then feel relaxed, and thus have restful and restorative sleep.

If you want to learn more about sleep from an Aware Parenting perspective, I invite you to read my book, *Sound Sleep and Secure Attachment with Aware Parenting*.

### *Inner Loving Mother* and *Inner Loving Father* phrases

I love you when you're playful.

I love joining in with your play.

I have so much energy to join in with your play.

Your energy is not too much for me.

I love all of your energy.

I welcome your energy.

I love seeing you being funny.

I love having fun with you.

I'm here to follow your lead.

I trust that you know what you need to be able to go to sleep.

I'm here to help you with what you need to go to sleep.

I will stay close with you when you go to sleep.

I will never judge you or shame you when you're silly and goofy.

I love you when you're being silly and goofy.

I trust that you know exactly what you need.

I love you.

## CHAPTER SIX

# When a child isn't going to sleep

*I just can't go to sleep, Dad. I'm so tired, but somehow, I just can't go to sleep. I really, really want to. I know you think I'm doing this deliberately. You got so angry tonight and I can see that you think I'm doing this on purpose, but I just feel all antsy.*

*You leave me alone and I just don't know what to do. I don't know how I can get to sleep. Sometimes it's like I'm here forever, all on my own, awake for a hundred years. I put my thumb in my mouth and it seems to help, but not really.*

*What's this? You and Mum come into my room, and you're holding hands.*

*"We're sorry that we left you alone to go to sleep," you say. "We're not going to do that again until you're ready for us to leave you. We're going to stay with you until you fall asleep."*

*It's a good thing you got me a big bed for sleepovers, because you get in one side, Mum, and Dad, you get in the other side, and already my body feels kind of different. I ask if I can hold one hand each, and you both say yes. You start telling me a story about when I was born, and what happened when I was a little baby, and how happy you were that I was here.*

*I don't know what's happening, but some tears are coming out of my eyes and down the sides of my face. I feel really sad. Usually, I need to hold in my tears, cos of those times you told me there was nothing to cry about Dad, and Mum, when you told me I was okay.*

*But I don't feel okay, whatever that is. I feel sad.*

*And I do have something to cry about.*

*I don't really know what it is, but I know there's something.*

*My crying spreads to my throat and my heart and I start to sob. You both move closer, giving me a kind of sandwich hug, and I cry and cry and cry. "We're here, sweetheart, we're listening. You're letting it all out," you say, Dad. That helps me cry more. You love me, you really love me. I feel so safe in between you, like the crying is all coming out but I'm safe here, and warm, and you really do love me.*

*"We love you so much," you say, Mum. I cry like a waterfall, all the tears are raining down and down and down. The tears and snot have flooded the world. But I'm safe here with you.*

*And it's so weird, because the tears have all come out, and now I feel sleepy, and I also know that I'm going to be able to fall asleep. Who knew how easy it could be!*

*I sigh, and yawn, and I feel all this love in my body. I cuddle up into our cuddle puddle, and I feel my eyes drifting closed, so safe and sound.*

*Nighty night, Mum and Dad. I love you.*

## About children who aren't going to sleep

Children want to sleep when they're **tired** (unless they haven't had the connection they want with us during the day, and they're staying up to have more connection), but they also need to feel *safe* and *relaxed* to be able to go to sleep.

**Safety:** The younger they are, the more likely it is that they will need *closeness* in order to feel safe enough to fall asleep.

**Relaxation:** When they are tired, children have less ability to suppress painful accumulated feelings. Those feelings tend to bubble up to be felt, expressed, and released, so that children can feel deeply relaxed and can sleep restfully and restoratively.

Often, we do things to help them feel relaxed, but if after doing those things, they still can't sleep, it's likely that we may have overridden their natural relaxation response – which is to laugh and play, cry and rage, or talk about their feelings[4], all with our loving support. It's the tension from accumulated feelings that prevents them from feeling relaxed enough to sleep.

With practice, we can discover what they need and follow their lead, whether that's joining in with their play and following their giggles, or listening to them share about their day, or staying with them while they cry and rage and release painful feelings and tension from their bodies. Their bodies are so wise.

If you want to learn more about sleep from an Aware Parenting perspective, I invite you to read my book, *Sound Sleep and Secure Attachment with Aware Parenting*.

---

4   Talking becomes more important as a method of expression and release as children get older but doesn't ever completely replace the release power of crying, raging, and laughter (without tickling).

## *Inner Loving Mother* and *Inner Loving Father* phrases

I'll stay with you when you go to sleep for as long as you need me to.

I know how natural it is for you to want to be close with me before bed.

I love you exactly as you are.

I love being close with you.

I love listening to your feelings.

I'm here to listen to whatever you want to share with me.

I love to hear about your day.

There's nothing you could share that would change my love for you.

I love you unconditionally.

I'm here to help you feel deeply relaxed.

I know how much you want to sleep when you're tired.

I welcome all of your feelings.

I love you so much.

# SECTION 2

# Challenging Situations

CHAPTER SEVEN

# A parent moving in to protect a child from getting hurt

*Oh, here it goes again. My sister, Sally, is coming for me. She's got that look on her face and I know that something's gonna happen. I hear you in the kitchen, Mum. Sally's got my blue car in her hand – the one that I got for my last birthday, and she's smiling in that way she does. What's it gonna be this time? Throwing it and breaking it? Trying to hit me with it? I've seen it all before, and yet again, I'm on my own with it.*

*But what's this, Mum?*

*You come in, and you look at me, and then at Sally, and you somehow see what's about to happen. You get in between us, just as Sally lifts her hand. Oh, she's going to throw it! Not my blue car!*

*But in that moment, you put your hand out, Mum, and you hold her hand and my car, and you stop her from throwing it. Wow!*

*"I'm not willing for you to throw the car, because I'm here to keep everyone safe. And I'm right here and listening." You turn around to face me, "And I'm here with you, too, sweetheart. I'm here to keep everyone safe. I'm here to protect your things. I'm here and listening to you too."*

*This has never happened before. You've always left me to it.*

*All at once, Sally starts shouting stuff at you. I don't know what kind of magic beans you've eaten, but you're all calm. You keep hold of Sally's arm and the car, and you listen to her, but then turn to me, too. I see you look in my eyes, and nod. "I'm here to keep you safe, sweetheart. I'm not willing for her to hurt you or break your things."*

Chapter Seven: A parent moving in to protect a child from getting hurt

*That does it. Someone pulls out the plug of the bath of water and my eyes fill up with tears. You really are here to protect me this time. You're keeping me safe. A million years of tears fall out of my eyes and I cry and cry and cry. It's like more magic, because Sally's raging and I'm crying and you're here with us both. You're keeping me safe from her, but you're staying with us both.*

*"I see you, sweetheart. I'm here. I'm listening," you say to me. You turn and say something similar to Sally.*

*Wow. It's so LOUD in here! But I still feel safe, and I keep crying and crying. I remember all the times my sister hurt me or broke my stuff and you didn't come and protect me or help me. I think about that time when she broke the cup and then blamed me. I cry and I cry and I cry. The bathtub was so full of water, and it's all coming out. Who even knew that I could cry so much? Sally's going for it too. But I know you've got us, Mum. We're both safe here with you.*

*My bathtub's getting emptier and Sally's volcano is getting quieter. The blue car has been on the floor for ages.*

*Somehow we all end up snuggled on the sofa, me under one of your arms and Sal under the other. We're both quiet now, apart from some sighs.*

*You speak up. "I'm sorry for all the times that I didn't come in to help you both and keep you both safe. I'm here to listen to any feelings about that you want to tell me about. From now on, I'm doing things differently. Call out whenever you need help and I will come to support you both."*

*I start to tell you about what happened, and Sally joins in, and somehow she's not the enemy any more. And she's not being yucky to me either.*

*Wow, Mum, this really is magic. Maybe she doesn't hate me after all. We cuddle up on the sofa together and you read us a book. I feel so different. I feel all relaxed and sleepy.*

*I feel so much bigger, too!*

*My whole world looks different now.*

## About moving in to protect a child from being hurt

Children need the support of adults to protect them and keep them safe when there are fights between siblings or friends, especially if there's any physical threat. That's part of us creating physical and emotional safety for them.

It's our role as parents to help them be safe when they are too young, physically or emotionally, to be able to protect themselves. It's also our responsibility to listen to the feelings of both children if we didn't get there in time to stop the hurting or destruction from happening, so they can heal from the experience.

A child who is doing the hurting is in as much need of loving listening as a child who has been hurt. Aggressive behaviour is generally caused by painful unexpressed feelings.

One of the aspects of Aware Parenting is to protect our children from stress and trauma wherever possible, and to support them to heal from all the inevitable stress and trauma that does happen. That happens through them using their innate healing responses of crying and raging along with vigorous movement, laughter and play, and therapeutic talking. They need to feel safe in the present, with the support of a loving listener, for that to happen.

If you want to learn more about mediation between siblings, and using *Loving Limits*, I invite you to read *Cooperative and Connected* by Aletha Solter, PhD, and my book, *I'm Here and I'm Listening*.

### *Inner Loving Mother* and *Inner Loving Father* phrases

I'm sorry for all the times I didn't step in to keep you safe.

I'm here to listen to all the feelings you felt at those times.

It's my responsibility to step in to protect you until you're big enough to do that yourself.

I'm here to keep you safe.

I love you.

I'm here with you.

I see how powerful you are.

And I see when you need help.

I'm always here to help.

I love helping you.

I will always help when you ask for help.

I'm here to protect you when you need me.

I'm not willing for you to be hurt by others.

I'm so sorry for all the times I wasn't here when you needed me.

I'm here now.

I love you.

I'm listening.

## CHAPTER EIGHT

# Leaving the park

*Uh oh, Dad, I see you in the corner of my eye, and your leg is doing that tapping thing that tells me you're getting fed up. Why does that happen EVERY time we go to the park? I love it so much here! I feel so much freedom. One of the things I love the most is swinging on the swing as HIGH as I can go! I feel SO free! I like to sing at the same time. It's like I'm flying. Yes, I'm like a big bird, like one of those big eagles, flying so high. I swing and I swing and I'm free and big and I can move so far and so fast! I LOVE it!*

*I also love climbing to the very, very top of the witch's hat. Eagle me likes being able to look down and see everything. Everyone looks so small. Even you look small, Dad, down there, on your phone. I look around me. I look above me. I see the trees and the clouds and I can breathe. I sigh. I could stay here forever, in my eagle nest. It's so different to how I feel at school. I'm so small there.*

*I look down again. I expect you'll be telling me to get down so we can go home. It's aways the same.*

*But what's going on? You're climbing up. I've never seen you do that before! Wow, Dad! What are you going to do when you get up here? Are you coming to get me down?*

*You arrive at the rope below me, and you look around you, and smile. "What a view from here!" you say. Hmmm. That's new. We sit silently together for a while.*

*"I'm an eagle, and I can see the whole world from here," I try out.*

*"Hello eagle friend," you reply. "I'm just a little bird, but I love being high up here with you. But I don't think I could ever be as high as you," you say.*

Chapter Eight: Leaving the park

*I'm a bit shocked, Dad. You're so serious most of the time. Either that, or you're always trying to show me how much bigger and more powerful than me you are. This is so new!*

*"I'm the biggest eagle around here," I say.*

*"I can see how big you are," you reply.*

*This goes on, and I start to laugh. I love being a big eagle, bigger than you. This is fun!*

*"Well, I'm the eagle and I'm the boss, and I say we're going to fly to the swings now!"*

*I wonder if you'll follow me?*

*I jump down the witch's hat, and pretend to fly to the big swings. I reckon you won't do that. But, what!? You pretend to fly too! Oh Dad, this is fun!*

*I get on the swing and I swing as high as I can, and you join in next to me. We fly SO high and I start to say, "Weeeeeeeee!" and "Woohoooooo!" and you copy me. Well, this is turning out very different, today! I laugh out loud with joy. I love this so much!*

*I jump off the swing, and I start to fly around the park, and yes, Dad, you follow me! We fly together, around and around, through the tunnel, and over the other climbing frame. I'm laughing and you're laughing and this is so great!*

*We fly around forever. Time goes on and it's as if we've been here a thousand years.*

*Finally I hear, "Eagle, eagle, this little bird is ready to go back to our nest for some dinner," from you. I'm so happy to follow you as we fly towards the car, swooping and swerving. Eagle me is hungry too. On the way home we talk about eagles and how big and free they are. I can still feel the eagle in me. I feel big, and free, as if I have so much space inside of me and all around me.*

*I'm happy to go home with you, Dad.*

*Let's do this again soon!*

## About play and cooperation

Play is an incredibly powerful part of childhood. Through play, children practice what's required for them to learn in the culture they're growing up in. They can also process experiences that they've had, and heal from stressful or traumatic situations.

In Aware Parenting, these special forms of play are called *attachment play*, after the book of the same name by Aletha Solter, PhD, Founder of Aware Parenting. I highly recommend reading it if you want to understand more about the power of *attachment play*.

If we join in with their play, particularly if we take on the less powerful position and be mock-scared, mock-angry, or mock-surprised (called power-reversal games in Aware Parenting), we can help them feel more powerful, which is key to healing from stress or trauma and being willing to cooperate.

In addition, *attachment play* helps parents and children feel more connected with each other, as this story above shows. When children feel more connected with us, they are often more willing to cooperate with us. It really can work like magic!

## *Inner Loving Mother* and *Inner Loving Father* phrases

I'm sorry for all the times I didn't come and play when you asked me to.

I'm here to listen to all the feelings you felt when I didn't join in with your play.

I'm listening to however you felt when I told you to "be serious" or to "stop being silly."

I'm so sad that I said things like that to you.

I'm so willing to play what you want to play.

I love playing the games that you choose to play.

I love seeing you have fun.

I love having fun together.

I will always say "yes" when you ask me to play.

I love learning what you're interested in.

I love being silly and goofy together.

I feel so happy seeing you happy.

I'm willing to keep playing for as long as you want me to.

I love being present with you.

I love you.

## CHAPTER NINE

# When a child isn't cooperating

You're always asking me to do stuff, Mum, and it's all things that don't mean anything to me. I don't care about brushing my teeth. I like wearing my clothes to bed. I don't care what my hair looks like. Why do you want me to do all these things every day? I just want to play and have fun. I've got so many important things going on in my life. I've been setting up this amazing pirate world with all my plastic bricks and wooden blocks and I think it's so cool. And you always just want me to tidy it up. I don't want it to be all tidy. I like it just as it is. And I needed to get everything off the shelves today because I couldn't find the pirate captain that I just really wanted for this game.

Oh, here you come. I know that you're going to get all serious and tell me to put it all away. But I don't WANT to put it all away! I want to keep playing with my pirates. They're just about to find a new world, and it's so fun!

Hang on! You turn around and you've got an eye patch on! It's that one I wore for Halloween last year! I forgot all about it! "Ahoy there, captain! First mate Mummy here to sign in for duty!" This is so weird, Mum. Weird, but I love it! I smile a bit, not knowing what you're going to do next! You're talking in a funny pirate voice and I'm starting to laugh. You really do get how much I love pirates, then! I just love all their adventures! I feel so excited and happy when I play pirate games, cos there are new things that are going to happen and they're going to be fun!

"What do you want me to do, Captain?" you ask. I tell you where to put the red blocks and you do it, exactly how I want you to. This is so fun. I love that you're doing what I want.

*Next, I tell you how to make the pretend sea with the blue wrapping paper with fishes on it that we saved from my birthday. And you do it! Wow!*

*We're having so much fun together!*

*After a while, you say, "Captain, I'd love your help with all this treasure here. I've got this treasure chest (you point to the shelves) and I want to put all the gold and jewels and diamonds into it. Are you willing to help me?"*

*I know what you're doing, cos this is all the stuff I took off the shelves earlier on, but I don't even care, cos I actually want to help you put it all back again. Plus, you're singing this fake pirate song and you're making the words all funny, and I'm laughing and singing along! I pretend it's all treasure, and together we put it in the treasure box. I'm pretty surprised, cos I always thought tidying up was boring, but doing it together and pretending it's treasure is actually kind of fun. I like choosing where each bit of treasure goes! And we do it all. Wow. That was a lot of treasure!*

*"Captain, I have a new mission. We have a new ship ready. Would you like to come and see if it's up to your pirate standards?" you say. I'm pretty sure you want me to come and get into the bath, but I find myself happily coming along. We sing sea shanties all the way. And yes, it's the bath, and you turn on the taps. I brought some of the plastic pirates and we carry on with the game. They even help me brush my teeth and put on my PJs.*

*"I had so much fun playing pirates with you today, Mum."*

*"I did too, sweetheart," you say.*

*Tidying up isn't so bad, after all!*

## About cooperation

Just like us, children are more likely to cooperate if they feel connected, and if they have a sense of agency, choice, and fun in doing what we've asked.

Bringing in *attachment play* (based on the book of the same name by Aletha Solter, PhD) when we're wanting a child to cooperate with us can often bring really surprising results. Not least being that we might find that we have so much more fun, too!

If you want to learn more about eliciting cooperation with Aware Parenting, I invite you to read *Cooperative and Connected* by Aletha Solter, PhD, and *I'm Here and I'm Listening* by me.

### *Inner Loving Mother* and *Inner Loving Father* phrases

I'm so sorry for all the times that I told you what to do and punished you when you didn't do what I asked.

I'm here to listen to all of your feelings about that.

You have as much right to say no as I do.

Of course you felt powerless or angry when I made you do things.

I welcome all of your feelings about that.

I'm so willing to ask you to do things in more fun and exciting ways.

I'm so willing for us to have more fun together.

I love connecting with you.

I love hanging out with you.

I love doing all the everyday things that we do together.

I appreciate you every time you cooperate with something I ask.

Your needs are as important as mine.

I'm willing for us both to get our needs met.

I love you.

CHAPTER TEN

# When a child asks for lots of things but actually needs to cry

*I feel all funny in my tummy, Mummy. I don't know what's happening. I don't know what I want. I want some cereal. Oh Mummy, you're here, and you make me some cereal.*

*I come over, and I look at the cereal, but I still feel all funny when I look at it. That's not it. I don't like that bowl.*

*I want the pink bowl, instead.*

*You go and tip the cereal into the pink bowl.*

*I look at it, but I still feel all funny in my tummy. I want some milk, Mummy. Can you put the oaty milk on it for me, Mummy? I want the oaty milk.*

*You pour on the oaty milk, and I look at it, and I don't know what's happening to me, but I feel even more funny.*

*"I don't WANT the oaty milk. I want the cow milk, Mummy."*

*You bend down next to me, and something different is happening now.*

*"I really hear that you want the cow milk, sweetheart, and I'm not willing to get you another bowl of cereal with the cow milk, because we don't have much cereal left and I want everyone else to be able to have some too. And I'm here and I'm listening, lovely."*

*All at once, the funny feeling comes out of my tummy, up and out of my mouth and nose and eyes.*

"BUT I WANT THE COW MILK!" I shout.

"I really hear that you want the cow milk, sweetie, and I'm not willing to get you any right now, and I'm here and I'm listening."

The funny feeling gets bigger and bigger, until it's a red storm all around me.

"I WANT THE COW MILK!"

"I hear you, sweetheart. Not right now. I'm here and listening."

The red storm becomes a red volcano.

"RAAAAAAAARRRRRGHHHHHHHH!" I shake my head, I stamp my feet, I lash out. I become a raging red tornado. "IT'S NOT FAIR! I WANT IT!"

You're there, nodding.

I become the raging roaring red tornado. Red dust flies out of me everywhere. I roar and I rage.

I rage and I roar.

And you stay there, Mummy. You stay there, and when I look through the dust storm for a moment, I see your eyes, and they're warm, and I can feel the love, and my roaring and raging get louder and louder.

I'm the biggest, loudest, reddest, ragiest dust storm there ever was. I'm red forever. My red dust takes over the world, but you're there, you're there Mummy, and you're not red.

I rage and I rage and I rage and I rage. Oh, this was the funny feeling. This was what was underneath. It all makes sense now.

I feel so powerful now. I'm the most powerful red dust storm the world has ever seen. I keep letting it all out. The red comes out and out and out and out. I've even forgotten what it was I wanted.

Then there's less red. There's not so much red in me now, Mummy.

Then the red is all gone. It's all gone now, Mummy.

*And next is blue.*

*The blue is rain. I rain and rain and rain. I cry and cry and cry. I fall into your arms, Mummy, and you are there. You are not the blue. I am the blue and I cry and cry and cry. I'm blue forever. I'm the bluest blue that ever was. I'm blue to the end of the world. I'm sobbing and crying.*

*Oh, this was the funny feeling, next to the red.*

*The blue is going away, and now there's the yellow.*

*I am the yellow sun. The blue is gone, and I am warm. I am the sunshine after the rain. I feel so warm in your arms, Mummy. I look up to your face, and I see you smiling down at me. I see the love in your eyes. We smile together. "I love you, Mummy," I say.*

*"I love you too, sweetheart," you reply.*

*We talk for a bit, and then I can feel a different feeling in my tummy. I am hungry, after all. "I'd like that cereal now, Mummy. I love the oaty milk. You choose the spoon, Mum, I don't mind which one it is."*

*We sit together at the table, all eating breakfast, on a yellow kind of day. Yum! This cereal is so yummy!*

## When a child asks for lots of things but really needs to cry

When children have *healing-feelings*[5] bubbling away that they're trying to express, they will often try to find pretexts on which to place those feelings. We may also do this as adults!

We can usually tell if a child is (unknowingly) trying to find a pretext to express their painful feelings, rather than just needing choice. If they keep asking for things, and when we give them what they've requested they're not happy with it, this is a signal that there are *healing-feelings*

---

5  *Healing-feelings* is a term that I created to differentiate the feelings from *needs-feelings*. This is not an official Aware Parenting term. *Healing-feelings* are feelings that need to be felt, expressed, and heard. In contrast, *needs-feelings* are feelings that indicate unmet needs. When the need is met, the feelings dissipate.

driving the urgency. This often happens over and over, with different items being requested.

They're trying to find what I call an *'emotional coat hanger'*[6] upon which to hang their feelings. Once we realise that they don't have a need that they're trying to meet, and they are actually trying to express some painful feelings, we can offer them a *Loving Limit*[7], where we communicate our unwillingness to keep trying to fix things, and show and tell them that we're there to listen to their feelings.

If we keep the focus on the thing that they're using as the pretext for the feelings, while holding in mind that the feelings aren't really much to do with it at all, this often helps. In this example, the mother tells the child that she isn't willing to get more cereal, even though she knows that the feelings aren't really about the cereal. In that way, the child is most likely to be able to express the painful feelings that they are trying to let out.

If you want to learn more about how children use pretexts to let out painful feelings, and how to offer *Loving Limits*, I invite you to read my book, *I'm Here and I'm Listening*.

---

6   Another term I created which is not an official Aware Parenting term.
7   A term I created to describe what already existed in Aware Parenting, and which is now an official Aware Parenting term.

## *Inner Loving Mother* and *Inner Loving Father* phrases

I'm here to understand what's really going on for you, sweetheart.

I'm here to be a safe space for you to express your feelings.

I welcome all your feelings.

I welcome your rage and your sadness.

I welcome your frustration and overwhelm.

I'm here to listen to it all.

I'm saying no, and I'm here to listen to everything you feel when you hear me say that.

I welcome all of your feelings.

Your feelings are beautiful gifts.

I'm here to love you.

I'm here to listen to you.

I love you, sweetheart.

## CHAPTER ELEVEN

# When a child is doing things that the parent asks them not to

*I'm all sharp and spiky. I'm a walking hedgehog, an anteater, an echidna. Don't come near me, or I'll spike you.*

*You're here watching TV, Dad, as I walk into the room. You never take any notice of me, so you won't care what I'm doing.*

*I'm sharp and spiky. I look around me. Your laptop is on the table. I go over to it, looking over towards you, to see if you notice me.*

*You look up from the screen. "Hi, love, how are you?"*

*I keep walking. I open the lid and start bashing the keys. I look back over towards you and I slowly smile, a very big grin. You've asked me so many times to not play with your laptop.*

*I see your eyebrows scrunch as they always do. I know what's coming next. The usual.*

*I look back at the keys I'm still bashing, feeling the smile on my face still.*

*I look up again.*

*But what's this? Your eyebrows aren't scrunched. You look different.*

*I don't get it.*

*You walk over to me. This is it. This is where you start yelling. See if I care. I'm so spiky, you'll never get in, whatever you do.*

*My ears wait.*

Chapter Eleven: When a child is doing things that the parent asks them not to

*But what's this?*

*There's no yelling.*

*I look down, and I see your hand slowly coming over on top of mine.*

*"I'm not willing for you to hit the keys like that, love, because I want to protect my laptop from getting broken. And I'm here and I'm listening."*

*That's weird. What, no punishing? No shouting? No telling me, "It's not funny!?"*

*I look up and smile again, and try to keep bashing. That will DEFINITELY do it.*

*I look into your eyes, a cold hard stare. My spikes are the spikiest they've ever been. My smile is the biggest smile in the world.*

*Your hand comes down with more pressure. It doesn't hurt me, but I can feel it.*

*"Love, I'm really not willing for you to hit the keys, and I'm right here with you. I'm listening."*

*The tight string inside me snaps.*

*"I HATE YOU!" I rage.*

*You'll be destroyed by my spikes. Or you'll destroy me.*

*But nope, there's really something going on here. You don't snap. You don't bite. I feel this warmth and calm coming from you. Something happens to my heart, to my spikes, to my mouth.*

*"You just never get it, do you Dad?"*

*"I'm here and I'm listening, love. I'm here to listen to you."*

*That does it. The spikes shatter and explode.*

*"YOU NEVER LISTEN TO ME. I HATE YOU SOOOO MUCH!"*

*I rage and I rage.*

*You aren't destroyed. You aren't spiked. You stay, hand out, warm eyes, soft jaw. You really are here, Dad. You really are listening.*

*I rage and I rage. Inside the spikes there's all this hate and anger and noise and I'm here. I'm here. And you're here with me.*

*Inside my spikes keep spewing it all. I'm letting it all out, Dad. It's all been inside, and now you're here and listening.*

*I am SO angry. My spikes have been keeping me safe. I'm SO angry.*

*I rage some more.*

*And then the spikes are dissolving.*

*And here is the soft belly of hedgehog me.*

*A sob bursts out of my soft tummy. I cry and cry and run into your big strong arms.*

*You hold me.*

*You hold me, Dad, and you murmur soft words into my hair as I cry and I cry and I cry. I let it all out.*

*I didn't even know this was here. I didn't know. I didn't know, Dad. I didn't know I could cry this much. But I keep on crying and crying.*

*My soft belly is here, against yours. I look up, and you smile.*

*"Hi!" you say.*

*"Hi, Dad."*

*We keep hugging for a really long time. Finally, I'm ready to go and sit on the sofa with you.*

*"Want to tell me anything?" you offer.*

*"Yes...." I respond, and I tell you. I tell you all of it.....*

## When a child keeps doing something that the parent asks them not to do

Parents can often feel confused when their child seems to deliberately do things they know we don't want them to do.

In old parenting paradigms, we might tell ourselves that they're *"being disrespectful"* or *"not taking us seriously"*, especially if they're smiling or laughing at the same time.

However, from an Aware Parenting perspective, we can trust that they are doing it because they have painful feelings and are needing help to let those feelings out. The smiling/laughter is an expression – and release – of fear.

We can move in with a *Loving Limit,* and with compassion, say no to the behaviour and yes to the feelings causing the behaviour, just as the dad did in this story. When we listen lovingly to the painful feelings that they have been unknowingly asking for our help to release, our child can come out the other side, having released the pain. They will feel relaxed and connected again, naturally wanting to cooperate and contribute.

If you want to learn more about *Loving Limits*, I invite you to read my book, *I'm Here and I'm Listening*.

### ***Inner Loving Mother*** and ***Inner Loving Father*** phrases

I will always see you through the eyes of love.

I will always look for the true reason behind your behaviour.

I'm here to really understand you, sweetheart.

I won't judge you or your behaviour.

I'm here to keep you safe.

I can take care of my own feelings and my own needs.

I know that your behaviour is a cry for help.

I'm here to understand what's really going on for you.

I'm always willing to hear what you really need.

I welcome all of your feelings.

I'm here to help.

I love you, sweetheart.

I love you unconditionally.

CHAPTER TWELVE

# When a child is on a screen

*Here we go again, Dad. You've got that judgy look on your face. What will it be this time? Going on about what gaming does to my dopamine? Or my eyesight? Maybe you're going to go on about how I should spend more time outside, like what you did when you were a kid. And then you get angry if I don't get off straight away.*

*I wish you understood how much I love this. I'm right in the middle of this new level, and it takes all my concentration to get to this point. I've already needed to go back to the start three times, and I really want to get to the next level this time. But I guess you'll get judgy and tell me to get off and you won't even care about what I'm doing, as usual.*

*You come and sit next to me, and I'm waiting, just waiting, for the orders, while trying to go as fast as I can so I get to the next level.*

*It takes me some moments to realise that you're not saying anything. You're watching what I'm doing.*

*Huh.*

*That's new.*

*I keep playing. I'm so close to the end of the level. I'm so excited. It's taking all my concentration. This is such a tricky part and I read on another forum about this trick I can do at this point.*

*"I DID IT! WOOHOOOO!" I turn around, and you offer me a high five! "YOU DID IT!" you say! Wow, Dad! I'm so surprised, and kind of happy, to hear you say that. You're celebrating me? I thought you hated gaming. I tell you that.*

*"I'm sorry that I've been so judgy, love. I'm not going to do that any more. I see that you love doing this and I want to learn more about what you love about gaming. Perhaps you'd even teach me some?"*

*"Sure, Dad, how about now? There's a new game I want to try out so we can both be beginners on it!"*

*"I'd love that!"* you say. Wow! I'm excited! I've been longing for you to be interested in this, and I felt so hurt when you judged me.

I just want you to see me and understand me and what I love.

## When children are on a screen

Screens are such a charged topic, and I invite each parent to listen in to themselves deeply in relation to screens and their parenting values.

***However, if your child really loves a show or a game, being interested in what they're interested in can make a huge difference to them.***

Just as we might love sharing about a book we've read or a movie we've watched, or a hobby we're into, children's needs for acceptance, mattering, and being understood can be deeply met when we ask questions about what they're doing and are interested in their responses.

Joining in and watching or playing can deepen the connection. Finding ways to have fun together with screens can also make a big difference to them and how they feel.

If you want to learn more about Aware Parenting and screens I invite you to read my book, *I'm Here and I'm Listening*.

## *Inner Loving Mother* and *Inner Loving Father* phrases

I'm sorry for judging you when you were on a screen.

I'm not willing to judge you any more.

I'm sorry for not understanding your experience.

I'm really willing to understand what you love.

I'm sorry for telling you to just get off.

I see how much you're enjoying this.

I want to know more about what you enjoy.

I'd love to watch with you.

I'd love to play the game with you.

I care about you.

I'm interested in you.

I care about what you're interested in.

What you're interested in matters to me.

I want to know about what you love.

You are so important to me.

I love you.

# SECTION 3

# Suppression of Feelings

## CHAPTER THIRTEEN

# Helping a child unfreeze

*I'm a block of ice in a cold, cold world. I'm so far away. I see you over the other side of the playground, Mummy, but it's like you're in a different world. I'm here but I'm not here.*

*You come over and touch my hand, but it's cold. I'm still as cold as ice. You take my hand and I go with you, an ice robot, as we walk home together. Ice, ice, it's all I know. I'm so cold. I'm a cold robot.*

*We get home and I sit down and stare out the window.*

*You usually leave me alone when I'm like this. I think that you think that I'm calm. But I'm not calm, Mummy, I'm not calm at all. I'm cold. I'm lost. I need you. I need warmth.*

*You walk past, getting dinner ready. You smile, and I look away. I'm here, alone, a cold robot.*

*But what's happening, Mummy? You come back. You come and sit down next to me. "Hi, sweetheart," you say. You offer your arm, and I nod. I feel your arm around my shoulders, but I also don't feel it. I'm a block of ice. I'm frozen.*

*You speak to me, really quietly and gently. "I'm here with you, sweetheart. You're not on your own with this, now. I'm right here and I'm going to stay right here."*

*What's happening, Mummy? I can feel a bit of warmth in my shoulders and in my heart.*

*"You had a big day, lovely, didn't you? I'm right here with you now," you whisper in my ear. Even my ear feels a bit warm now.*

*Ice robot me relaxes a bit, and I sink over towards you, so you're holding me more. I can feel all the places where my shoulder and arm and tummy are touching your body. It's like you're the sunshine, starting to melt the ice. I can feel it happening. I can almost hear the cracking sound, like I saw when we watched that video about icy places together. I couldn't feel before, but now I can feel some warmth, and some melting ice, and some water.*

"I love you. I'm listening," you say.

*It's so funny, Mummy, because now I can feel the water in my eyes. I can feel my whole face wants to move. It doesn't want to be still any more. Some tears come out of my eyes. I can feel them running down my cheeks. I really am a melting ice block, Mummy!*

"I'm right here, sweetheart. I welcome all of your feelings," you speak.

*That seems to be some kind of warm magic key, because suddenly, big ice chunks break off. The melting is happening quickly, now. There's so much movement in me, but I can feel your stillness. My tears get so big, Mummy, and my mouth opens wide as I start to sob and cry. I'm big chunks of ice, melting and breaking. It's all breaking apart, and I'm water. I'm tears. I'm crying and crying.* "Mummy, Mummy, stay here with me."

"I'm staying right here with you, sweetheart. I'm right here. I'm not going anywhere."

*That does it. All the ice breaks apart and I'm so much water now, Mummy. I didn't know I had this much water in me. I cry and I cry and I cry and I cry. I cry all those frozen tears. I wail and I sob and there's all these loud noises coming out of me, Mummy.*

*And you just stay there with me, holding me. I can feel all your warmth. I am feeling so warm now too, Mummy. I'm not an ice robot any more. I'm a crying whale, swimming through the sea with you. I'm as sad as the whole ocean. My tears are as big as a whale. I'm crying like the whale. Wailing like the whale. I laugh a bit, Mummy! 'Wailing like a whale!' Get it? I don't even know how I can laugh in between the crying.*

*I go back to wailing again. And you're here, and you're here, and you're here. I'm the little whale, and you are the humungous big Mummy whale. I'm so safe with you, Mummy. We're whales together. This crying hurts, but I kind of like it too. I like feeling the warm and the water. I can feel my body again. I can feel me swimming in the sea, me and you. I can move. I am free.*

*I think all my tears have gone now, Mummy. I do this funny kind of sigh thing, and another one, and you're still holding me, Mummy. We're like whales going to the top of the sea, and jumping up in the air together. It's so funny, because I was frozen ice, and now I'm a big powerful whale. And we're here together. I look in your eyes and I smile at you. You smile back and I feel all this big warm open space around my heart. I think it's love! "I love you, Mummy!"*

*"I love you, sweetheart!"*

*We cuddle up together and I start to tell you about what happened today, and how I got to be that frozen robot.*

*I'm so glad that I'm a whale again, Mummy.*

## Helping children with unfreezing

Children can easily move into fight, flight, or freeze after events that can seem small to us. When they're in freeze mode, it can literally be like they're frozen. We might notice that they are really still, in a way that's quite different to being relaxed and present.

As parents, we might support them to come out of the frozenness through offering warmth; just like ice melts from the warmth of the sun, so too our child's freeze state will be melted into healing and connection by the warmth of our love. That love can be expressed through the warmth in our eyes, in our voice, in our touch.

When they feel physically and emotionally safe after receiving our warmth, we might see that the ice melts and transforms into the water of their tears. They might move into crying along with vigorous movements. These are all part of releasing the feelings and tensions from the past event, doing now what they needed to do at the time.

Offering the warmth of our loving presence can help them continue to cry so that they can release the whole chunk of feelings and come out the other side, feeling connected with themselves, their body, and us again.

If you want to understand more about Aware Parenting and how to help children move out of the freeze state (dissociation), I invite you to read *Healing Your Traumatized Child*, by Aletha Solter, PhD, and my book, *I'm Here and I'm Listening*.

**Inner Loving Mother and Inner Loving Father phrases**

I see when you're frozen, sweetheart.

I see you.

I understand what's happening for you.

You needed to freeze to be safe, sweetheart.

I'm here now, and I'm here to keep you safe.

I'm here with you.

I will keep on staying with you.

I won't leave you alone with these feelings.

I welcome all of your feelings.

I'm so comfortable with your tears and crying.

Your feelings are never too much for me.

My heart is as big as the world, able to hold you and your feelings.

I'm here and I'm listening.

I trust your timing for when you feel safe enough to feel and express those feelings. I'll still be here.

Your tears and your crying are so powerful and beautiful.

Your body is so wise.

I'm here and I'm listening.

I love you, however you feel.

CHAPTER FOURTEEN

# When a child is sucking their thumb

*I didn't like it when they laughed at me today when I was sucking my thumb. Why did they do that, Daddy? And why do you keep asking me to stop doing it? I can see that you get all grumpy when I do it and I don't know why. Why do you get all grumpy? Why don't you want me to do it? I'm lying in bed and I always have to suck my thumb before I go to sleep otherwise I just feel all antsy and I just can't sleep. I don't know why.*

*You come in, Daddy, and I'm expecting you to tell me it's time for bed and to go away again, but you come and sit next to me and tell me that you're sorry that you got grumpy about me sucking my thumb. Wow!*

*Then you ask me if I want to play a game with our thumbs, and I say yes, even though I'm not really sure what you mean.*

*You start being all silly, Daddy.*

*This is new! What's going on here?*

*I'm a bit unsure, but I join in. You're putting your thumb in your mouth and then pulling it out again and you're making funny noises each time. I kind of do the same thing and I giggle a bit.*

*Next you ask me what flavour my thumb is. What flavour? What do you mean? Oh, you're still playing the game. You tell me that yours is apple pie flavour, so I say that mine is chocolate ice cream. You pretend to taste my thumb, but you don't really, and then you say in a funny voice that it's poo flavour!*

*Oh Daddy, that is so funny! Did you really say "poo"? I'm laughing out loud now! You keep playing it over and over again. I put my thumb in again, and this time I say, "STRAWBERRY!" and again you make the poo joke. I don't know why this is so funny, Daddy, but it really is! I'm laughing so much now, and so are you! We laugh and we laugh and we laugh.*

*But what's this, Daddy? Suddenly my laughter changes and I'm like a big roaring lion.*

*I DIDN'T LIKE IT when they laughed at me today. And I DIDN'T like it when you got grumpy. I am SOOOO angry. I'm a raging roaring lion. I want to growl. I want to stamp my feet and push you away. I am the ANGRIEST lion in the world. I am angry angry angry. I rage and roar and rage and roar some more.*

*And you're here, Daddy, you're here with me. You're staying with me. I stomp and rage and roar some more and you're still here.*

*And then all the roaring is out.*

*I sit back down on the bed, next to you, and you give me a cuddle.*

*And then I start to cry. I feel so sad. I didn't like it when they laughed at me. I felt so alone. I felt so embarrassed. I didn't know what to do.*

*You listen. You listen, Daddy. You hold me while I cry. I let it all out.*

*Oh Daddy, I suddenly feel all sleepy and calm. I lie down next to you, and guess what, I feel all soft like a cloud. I don't need to suck my thumb to go to sleep, Daddy.*

*Wow!*

*Nighty night, I love you!*

# Thumb sucking

From an Aware Parenting perspective, thumb sucking generally indicates that a child is mildly dissociating from their feelings.

***We would never recommend pulling a child's thumb out of their mouth, nor trying to get them to take it out.***

Instead, we see their behaviour as a symptom that they have feelings bubbling up at that moment and they don't sense that those feelings are truly welcome at that time.

One of the ways we can help children feel more deeply connected with us and release some of their lighter feelings that thumb-sucking is holding in is through *attachment play*, explained in the book of the same name by Aletha Solter, PhD.

In this example here, the dad is using nonsense play – which is one of the nine types of *attachment play* – to help the child move out of dissociation and into releasing their feelings through laughter.

Once the child was feeling more connected with their dad and their body and feelings, the deeper feelings were free to come out and be heard, so that more healing could happen. First came the angry crying, then the sad crying. This led to a deep sense of presence and relaxation. This is a very common way that healing happens, but each child is unique and each process is different.

If you want to learn more about helping children move out of dissociation, I invite you to read *Healing Your Traumatized Child* by Aletha Solter, PhD, and my book *I'm Here and I'm Listening*.

ALL OF YOUR FEELINGS ARE WELCOME

***Inner Loving Mother* and *Inner Loving Father* phrases**

I love you when you're sucking your thumb, sweetheart.

I'm not willing for anyone to judge you or shame you when you're sucking your thumb.

I'm not willing for anyone to make you stop sucking your thumb.

I understand that you needed to suck your thumb.

I'm sorry for all the times I wasn't present with you when you needed to let your feelings out.

I'm here now, sweetheart. And I'm willing to listen to all of your feelings.

None of your feelings are too much for me.

I'm here and present with you.

And I trust your timing.

I trust that you will be ready in your own time to express those feelings.

I welcome all of your feelings.

I love you exactly as you are.

I'm here to help you know that you are safe to feel and express your feelings now, sweetheart.

I love you.

## CHAPTER FIFTEEN

# When a child is sucking on a dummy

*Mamma, I love my dummy. I want to hold it forever. Sometimes, I like to suck on one dummy and hold one at the same time. But Mummy, I want them nearly all the time now. I need them. I need them so much. But I also feel kind of like a wooden doll, all hard and stiff. I need them.*

*Mamma, I'm running to you and I fall over. Oh it hurts, Mamma. You are holding my dummy. I want it. Can I have it right now?*

*Oh but Mamma, you tell me not now. You say you don't think it's so helpful for me to have it right now. You say that you're listening.*

*But I NEED it. I need it right now. I start to cry and wail and scream. I NEED IT SO MUCH. It is my whole world.*

*But Mamma, you're there and you're staying and you're looking at me and I can feel you with me. You keep telling me that you're listening. I think I'm safe to keep crying and crying. I NEED MY DUMMY SO MUCH, Mamma. I need it. I feel all these feelings. I can feel. I'm feeling so much. I NEED my dummy, Mamma.*

*You stay right here with me, and I'm crying so much. I can feel all around my mouth. It's usually all hard and numb around my mouth, but I can feel my mouth all big and wide and I'm SCREAMING and I'm CRYING and I can feel it all.*

*It's so much, Mamma, it's so much. I feel so much. I thought you didn't want to listen to these feelings. You kept giving me the dummy. But this time you're not. You're listening and I'm crying and crying and crying.*

*It's funny, cos now I don't want my dummy any more. I kind of like crying, although it is ouchie too. But I like that my mouth and tongue are feeling more softy. They don't feel all ouchie like they do when I'm sucking on my dummy.*

*And oh what's this? My crying is stopping. I look up at you, and you're still there with me. You open your arms and I fall into them. We have the biggest hug.*

*Do you know what, Mamma? I actually do feel kind of different. Happier, and I'm calm without my dummy.*

*I feel all different. My mouth feels softer. My face feels all relaxed. Oh I like this!*

*Woweee! Mamma, will you come and play dragons with me now?*

## Sucking on a dummy

In Aware Parenting, dummies are seen as a way for children to suppress or mildly dissociate from feelings. If we want to listen to our child's feelings instead, we might approach it similarly to thumb sucking, and offer *attachment play*, which is described in detail in the book of the same name by Aletha Solter, PhD.

However, because we were the one who gave the dummy to them, unlike with thumb-sucking, which they chose to do themselves, we might offer a *Loving Limit*, which we do not recommend with thumb-sucking.

A *Loving Limit* is where we lovingly say no to the dummy, and yes to the feelings that the dummy is suppressing.

It's important to give the child information about why we are saying no to them having the dummy so they don't experience it as random power-over them. For example, we might say, *"I'm not willing for you to have your dummy right now, sweetheart, because I don't think it's the most helpful thing for you. And I'm right here and I'm listening."*

If you want to learn more about offering *attachment play* and *Loving*

*Limits* in response to thumb-sucking, I invite you to read my book, *I'm Here and I'm Listening*.

### Inner Loving Mother and Inner Loving Father phrases

I'm sorry that I gave you a dummy, sweetheart.

I thought it was the most helpful thing for you.

I didn't understand about listening to your feelings.

Now I understand.

Now I'm here to listen.

I welcome all your feelings, sweetheart.

I'm here to help you not need the dummy any more.

I love listening to your feelings.

I love you when you're crying.

I love you when you're raging.

I love you, however you feel.

# SECTION 4

# Aggression

## CHAPTER SIXTEEN

# When a child is hitting

*I might look like a cute puppy, but inside I'm a raging bull, and you don't even know it. Everything is wrong in my world. My legs and arms are all clunky. I'm looking for something to bash up against.*

*I'm just waiting for you to do something, anything, so I can push back at you. Surely I won't wait for long.*

*You walk past me on the way to the kitchen and you put your arm out to touch me on the arm.*

*That's it! THWACK! I hit you.*

*And I wait for the response. What will it be this time? "Be gentle," or "We don't hit in our family," or "It's not okay to hit"? Or perhaps you'll get all angry and I'll see that you'd like to thwack me back, even though you don't. What will it be? I kind of tense up more, waiting for whatever it is.*

*The pause tells me something's different this time.*

*I look up, unsure about what I'll see.*

*"Shall we dance?" you sing.*

*What?*

*"Shall we dance?" you keep singing.*

*You take hold of my hand that just hit you, and you reach out for the other one, and you start to pretend to dance.*

*"Oh, it's the waltz, is it?" you say, with a smile on your face.*

*What the heck is going on here, Mum?*

*I feel another surge from the raging bull, and I try to hit you again, but you've got my hand.*

*"Oh, we're rapping, are we? Shall we dance, shall we dance, shall we dance?"*

*You kind of swirl me around and I join in. This is the strangest thing ever, Mum, what TV show have you been watching?*

*Something's loosening in me.*

*But then the bull comes back. I try to kick you.*

*Somehow you manage to stop my foot with your hand, and then the singing happens again.*

*"Oh, hip hop, is it? Shall we dance, shall we dance, shall we dance?"*

*This is SO crazy, Mum. I don't know what on earth is going on, but I'm starting to smile. I'm becoming a dancing bull!*

*You keep dancing and singing, and it's like the red rag has gone.*

*I can see you again.*

*You're not a danger to me.*

*You keep going, and I start to join in. I'm even smiling and laughing a tiny bit. I ham it up and do big dance moves. Oh, I like how that feels. I'm doing big kicks with my legs, and big moves with my arms, and my body is starting to feel all together again.*

*I look up, smiling, and you're smiling at me.*

*We keep dancing around for ages and I feel SO different.*

*Phew! What a relief!*

*Thanks, Mum.*

## A child who is hitting

Sometimes, it will appear that children lash out for no reason, but from an Aware Parenting perspective, it's because they have painful feelings sitting in their body, waiting to be released. We could see those as a river of feelings, ready at any moment to overflow at the surface.

Another way of thinking about it is that they've been in fight or flight mode, and something in the present moment reminds them of a past experience, which sets off that fight response again.

With Aware Parenting, we have two options when responding to aggression. One is *attachment play*, and the other is *Loving Limits*.

We can only tell which one will be most helpful in the moment through experimenting with our child and observing what happens. This will tell us which will help them feel physically and emotionally safe at that time.

**When they experience that safety, they will be able to move out of the fight or flight response and to feel and express the feelings, which will help them move into resolution and then true calm.**

In this example, the mother moved in with *attachment play*[8], which helped the child feel a sense of safety and connection, so they could express and release the feelings through laughter, movement, and play.

Another example of *attachment play* in response to hitting is a power-reversal pillow fight. In this type of play, we play the less powerful role, being mock-surprised, mock-angry, or mock-scared in response to them repeatedly knocking us over. It's important that we keep ourselves safe when playing this game, so that although we make big exaggerated movements, pretending to fall over or fly backwards or jump in the air, we are finding a distance so that the thwacks from the pillow are not hurting us.

---

8  The 'Shall we dance?' game is one I made up, to the tune of a song of that name from the movie 'The King and I'.

Chapter Sixteen: When a child is hitting

# Power-reversal games are incredibly helpful for releasing feelings of powerlessness that are the root of aggression. If your child is laughing a lot during these types of play, they are releasing those kinds of feelings. When a child feels truly powerful, they don't need to be in fight or flight mode.

If you want to learn more about *attachment play*, I invite you to read *Attachment Play* by Aletha Solter, PhD, and my book, *I'm Here and I'm Listening*.

### *Inner Loving Mother* and *Inner Loving Father* phrases

I'm so sorry for all the times I judged you, shamed you, or punished you when you went to hit.

I'm sorry that I didn't get there in time to prevent you hitting.

It's my role to keep you safe, until you're able to do that for yourself.

I'm here to help you know deep in your body that you are safe now, and that you don't need to hit.

I'm here to love you and understand you, so you can stop hitting and feel those painful feelings instead.

I'm here to help you let out those feelings.

I'm here to laugh and play with you.

I'm also here to listen to your frustration and rage.

I trust that you know exactly how to feel and release these feelings.

Your body is so wise.

You are so wise.

ALL OF YOUR FEELINGS ARE WELCOME

I trust you.

I'm here with you.

I'll keep being here with you until you feel safe and calm again.

I love you, however you feel.

I love you, exactly as you are.

I love you, unconditionally.

CHAPTER SEVENTEEN

# When a child is throwing things

*Today, I hate the world. You said that I woke up on the wrong side of the bed, Daddy, but I don't know what that means. I do know that I am so grumpy. I hate my new shoes. I hate my breakfast. I hate that you rush me to have my breakfast. I hate it all. Hate, hate, hate it all.*

*Isn't it the weekend? Don't we ever get to go slowly? I hate the weekend.*

*You tell me to go and play. Well that sucks. I don't want to go and play. How can I play when I hate everything. I hate playing. Look at all these stupid things. I start doing a puzzle, but I can't do it. I hate puzzles.*

*I start building a big tower, but if falls down. I hate blocks.*

*You come over and ask me what I'm doing, and I've got this block in my hand, and I throw it. I pick up another one, ready to throw that too.*

*But you get here so quick, Dad, and you hold the block and my hand. What is going on?*

*"Hey love, I'm not willing for you to throw that, 'cause I'm here to protect our home from getting damaged. And I'm here, and I'm listening."*

*I don't like this.*

*I want to throw the block. I want to throw lots of blocks. I WANT to damage the house. I want to make holes in the walls. I want to smash things.*

*I try to move my hand, so I can throw the block at the mirror. But you keep holding it.*

*You don't let go.*

*"I WANT TO THROW THIS BLOCK!" I shout, as loud as I can.*

*"I hear you, love, I hear that you want to throw the block, and I'm not willing for you to throw it. And I'm right here with you. I love you, and I'm listening."*

*I want to smash the whole house up. I want to break you. I want to bash EVERYTHING.*

*"RAAAAAARRRRRGH!" I shout in your face.*

*My world is a tornado, and you are the calm centre of it.*

*"I'm here with you, love. I'm listening," you respond.*

*I become the biggest tornado the world has ever known. I want to damage everything. I want to break it all. I keep struggling with my hand, trying to throw the block at anything. I pick up another one with my other hand, ready to throw it. Somehow you see me, and you hold that hand and the block with your other hand.*

*"I'm not willing for you to throw the blocks, love. I'm right here with you. I'm here to keep us both safe. I'm here to protect our home. I love you and I'm listening."*

*That does it. The tornado is the tornadoeist it can be.*

*I roar in your face.*

*I tell you that I hate you.*

*I tell you I want to destroy everything.*

*But you keep being there, Dad. You are still the calm centre. Somehow, I know I'm safe. That I cannot destroy you, or our home. That you will keep me safe.*

*The tornado becomes a wild storm. There's rain now, heavy rain, big drops. I let go of the blocks, and you let go of my hands. I start to sob and wail. My heart is broken. My heart hurts SO much, Dad. I don't know if I can bear it.*

*You're standing in front of me still, and now your arms open wide, and*

*I fall into them, into the biggest hug I've ever had. We're both standing up, and I'm the wild storm still, and I cry and cry and wail, and I can feel all this pain in my heart. It really hurts, Dad.*

*It hurts so much. I hurt so much. I've been hurt so much.*

*But you're here with me, and I'm safe, and I can feel it. I can feel it all.*

*I keep crying, and you keep holding me, and I feel your big arms around me, keeping me safe. "I'm listening," you say. "I love you," you tell me. "I'm here to listen to it all," you express.*

*Oh Dad, when I hear you say those words, the storm becomes full-on rain. I'm raining and raining, and my tears are washing the world clean. All this pain, all this pain, Dad. I've been holding it all in, and now I'm feeling it all, and I'm letting it all out. I cry all the rain in the world, and you love me, and you're listening, and you understand.*

*The pain in my heart is going now, Dad, and the rain is stopping. I'm here in your arms and now I feel all warm and safe here.*

*I do these funny sigh things. I don't know what they are, but I feel all this space inside me.*

*The clouds are moving away and there's so much space all around me. I can really breathe. I feel all open in my chest, like a lovely breeze is flowing through me.*

*I can breathe, and I can feel, and my heart is all warm, and I'm cuddled up with you, and all is right with the world again.*

*I love you, Dad. I love you so much. My heart is a big bundle of love.*

## Children who are throwing things

When children are trying to throw things, it's often part of the fight or flight response. We can see the biological purpose of this – in times of danger, throwing a rock or a spear at a sabre-tooth tiger would have been really beneficial.

However, children will often be in fight or flight in situations where throwing isn't the most helpful response.

In Aware Parenting, our aim is to help them know that they are now physically and emotionally safe so that they no longer need to throw something to be safe. Then they can feel, express, and release the energy and feelings that were mobilised to keep them safe – often feelings such as anger and rage – so that they can return to a calm state of homeostasis.

*In order to do that, we need to be in a state ourselves where we feel safe, powerful, and loving, so we can prevent them from throwing, while helping them know that they are safe and loved, so they can move from the aggression to the expression.*

We can do that with *Loving Limits*, using the precise words that help us feel safe, powerful, and loving, and which support them to feel safe and loved. I love the phrase "not willing" but there is no official language for *Loving Limits* in Aware Parenting.

It is important that we also tell them *why* we're stopping their behaviour.

So, we're doing the minimum possible to stop the throwing, while communicating that we're here to keep them safe, that we love them, and that we're willing to listen to the feelings underlying the throwing.

I like phrases like, *"I'm not willing for you to throw, sweetheart, because I'm here to keep everyone safe/protect our home from damage, and I'm here and I'm listening."* I invite each parent to explore what language would help them most embody the *Loving Limit* and most help their child feel the safety to move into expressing the feelings rather than throwing.

If you want to understand more about hitting and the fight or flight response, and how to help children move out of that state, I recommend *Healing Your Traumatized Child* by Aletha Solter, PhD, and my book, *I'm Here and I'm Listening*.

### *Inner Loving Mother* and *Inner Loving Father* phrases

I see how many big feelings you are feeling, sweetheart.

I welcome all your big feelings.

I love you when you're feeling big feelings.

I love you when you're expressing big feelings.

I love you, whatever you do.

And I'm here to keep you safe.

I'm here to keep me safe.

I'm here to protect our home.

I can be with all of your feelings.

And I'm here to help you feel safe.

You're safe with me, sweetheart.

I'm not willing for you to throw things.

And I am willing to listen to all of your feelings.

I'm here with you.

I will keep on being here with you.

I love you so much.

## CHAPTER EIGHTEEN

# When a child is swearing

*I come through the front door and walk past you in the hallway, Mum. I drop my school bag and kick off my shoes. Urgh. You ask me about my day. "It was so shit," I whisper under my breath. That'll get you going. Serious Mum, lecturey-Mum will be here any moment. I've had enough of that crap at school all day, and now you're gonna give me more of it. I close my ears. I don't care what you say. It* was *shit.*

*Cos my ears are closed, I hardly hear what you say.*

*"Shit, split, scrit, flit, nit, wit, dit."*

*WHAT!!!*

*I pause, half way into my room.*

*"Shitty splitty flitty witty ditty kitty," you sing this time.*

*HANG ON A MINUTE. What the HELL is going on here? I come to a complete standstill, and start to turn around to face you, my eyebrows raising in the air. I slant my face to the side, a question mark on my face.*

*"Shitto blitto flitto itto snitto scritto," you say.*

*That does it. What on earth? A grin comes out. I can't stop it.*

*"SHITTY shitty CRAPPY crappy SO sucks, SO there!" I try out.*

*You kind of copy me, with even the pissed-offness, but you wiggle your eyebrows while you're doing it.*

*"SHITTY shitty CRAPPY crappy SO sucks, SO there!!" you respond, nodding your head, showing me that you understand.*

Chapter Eighteen: When a child is swearing

*Seriously, Mum. What on earth? I crack a smile.*

*I pretend I'm drumming this time, fake drumsticks in my hand.*

"So shit, so sucky, I hate it all and I'm not lucky."

*You start doing some kind of beatbox to it, so I keep going.*

"Shitty, crappy, it sucks so much."

"I'm not a rubber ducky," *you let out.*

*We both crack up! Rubber ducky! Oh Mum, I'm laughing so much, and you are too.*

"Rubby ducky, we're not lucky!"

*We are literally rolling around on the floor now, like that old fashioned ROFL people used to talk about.*

"Rubber ducky ducky ducky, not sucky or wacky," *you go on.*

*We literally have tears rolling down our cheeks now. My stomach actually hurts from laughing so much! I didn't know that laughter could be like this!*

*I look over at you, and you wiggle your eyebrows at me. That sets me off again.*

*Our laughter quietens down, and then I say,* "Lucky ducky!" *and we burst out laughing again. This could go on forever. I don't know if we'll ever stop.*

*Eventually, the laughter does come to an end, and you scoot over to me, so we're both sitting on the floor with our backs leaning against the wall.*

"Shit day, lovely?" *you say.*

*I grin.* "SO shit, Mum."

*And then I tell you all about it, and you really listen to me. You listen to it all. And somehow, after all that laughing, my body feels all peaceful, like a calm lake. I tell you about everything that happened, and some bubbles come up from underneath the lake. But you keep listening to me, and the lake gets calm again. I don't remember feeling this way before.*

*We go to the kitchen together and rustle up some snacks and we go back to our sitting on the floor position, and have a picnic together.*

*Wow, Mum. This was amazing. Thank you.*

## About swearing

When children are swearing, they might be doing it for a number of reasons, and it's our role to find the cause and tend to that, all from a stance of loving compassion.

They might be repeating what they heard, and trying to make sense of it.

They might have uncomfortable feelings, after having heard someone else swear – and they're needing to let out those emotions.

We might have reacted harshly when they swore in the past and they're trying to make sense of, and heal from, those experiences.

They might have some big feelings, and swearing helps them express the bigness of the feelings.

*Attachment play*, described in the book of the same name by Aletha Solter, PhD, is a helpful response to swearing. It helps children feel safe. It helps them feel loved. It helps them have a space to process whatever is going on for them, whether that's making sense of the swear words themselves, or why these words have so much power, or the feelings they felt hearing swear words, or the feelings they saw in us when we reacted, or, as in this case, releasing the feelings that the swearing is communicating.

Swearing is a symptom, and nonsense play, one of the nine types of *attachment play*, is one of the ways we can address what's underneath the symptom, and tend to it, so that the symptom doesn't need to be there any more, and so the swearing is no longer required. And if swearing comes back again, we can notice again what it really is: a flag for feelings.

## *Inner Loving Mother* and *Inner Loving Father* phrases

I'm sending love to you for every time you were judged or shamed for swearing, or saw that happening to others.

I'm here with you.

I love you when you're swearing.

I trust that there's an important reason why you're doing it.

I'm here to help with whatever that is.

I'm not willing to judge you when you're swearing.

I'm not willing to shame you when you're swearing.

I'm not willing for you to be judged, shamed, or punished by others when you're swearing.

I love you and I'm here to help you with whatever is going on for you.

There's nothing you could do that would push me away.

I've always got your back.

I'm always here when you need me.

I enjoy being playful with swearing with you.

I'll help you know the places and people where you're safe to swear, and the places where you might be met with harshness.

I'm here to keep you safe.

I'm so willing to be a safe space for you.

I love you unconditionally, exactly as you are.

## CHAPTER NINETEEN

# When a child is blaming others

There's a big dark cloud over my head, everywhere I go. It keeps following me, Dad. Bleurgh.

Oh I just bumped into you. That's YOUR fault, Dad. You did it.

You ask me where my bag is.

"I don't know. That's David's fault," I say. "He lost it."

I go and get some cookies from the cupboard and eat them. You come over and ask me if there are any left for you.

"I didn't do it. Mum didn't buy enough," I respond.

Everyone else is always doing things. I hate it. And yeah yeah, I know what's coming next. You always do that stupid lecture where you tell me to not be a victim, and to stop blaming people, and to be powerful. You say it's all my fault I'm a victim. How can that be my fault, Dad? You're the parent, not me.

I can't even be bothered to listen to the same old boring stuff. I get up from the table and start to walk away.

"But it isn't my fault that today is Friday!" you say.

HUH?

"And it wasn't me who just said that!" you go on.

Double HUH?

"In fact, I'm not Dad at all. YOU'RE Dad!" you let out, pointing at me.

*What on EARTH?*

*"And this isn't my mouth!"  you say, pointing to your mouth.*

*I can't help it. A smile starts to come on one side of my mouth. I stop it quickly.*

*"Well, it isn't my fault that I'm me," I respond. "You chose me to be here!"*

*You smile back.*

*"I'm not even me," the words come back from you, "I didn't do any of it."*

*"Well I definitely didn't do it. I didn't do any of it!" I say.*

*"Me neither!" you respond. "And it was definitely the dog who farted just now."*

*"It's ALWAYS the dog who farts, Dad!"*

*We both start laughing! I come over to you, and we keep on with the fart jokes and the 'it's not my fault' jokes.*

*I don't know how you did it, Dad, but that black cloud isn't there any more.*

*It's floating off into the distance.*

*"Want to come and play badminton?" you offer.*

*I nod, a big smile on my face, and we walk outside, hand in hand.*

*While we're playing, I start telling you about how Daniel said he doesn't want to be my friend any more. You listen, and you don't tell me what to do, or what I did wrong. You just really listen.*

*We keep playing, and I work out what to do. You didn't even tell me, Dad. I just worked it out!*

*Thanks, Dad! That was great!*

## When children are blaming

When children are blaming others for things, it often indicates that they're feeling powerless in some way, or they're scared about what would happen if they take responsibility, or show how powerful they are.

Sometimes, giving information can help them, but usually, the most helpful and healing responses are either *attachment play* (you can read more about this in the book of the same name by Aletha Solter, PhD) or listening to painful feelings that support them to express the powerlessness and rage underlying the blaming.

In the story above, the dad moved in with *attachment play* – nonsense play, to be specific. Without any trace of shaming or judgment, he helped his child release the powerlessness through laughter. The ongoing connection then helped the child to express more feelings, this time through sharing their experience in words.

Sometimes, *attachment play* won't be the apt response and *Loving Limits* will be more helpful, particularly if there's aggression and the child is blaming the other person. *Loving Limits* are when we say no to the behaviour and yes to the feelings causing the behaviour.

**When the child can release the powerlessness, as well as any frustration or rage, they can return to feeling more powerful again and won't need to blame others.**

### *Inner Loving Mother* and *Inner Loving Father* phrases

I hear that you're feeling powerless, sweetheart.

I understand that you want to blame others.

I welcome all your feelings, lovely.

I'm here with you.

Powerlessness feels so painful, doesn't it?

I'm listening to your powerlessness.

I'm here with your fear.

I welcome your rage.

I see your power.

I'm here to help you know how powerful you are.

I trust your timing.

I'm here to help you know you're safe when you're powerful.

I love you, sweetheart.

## CHAPTER TWENTY

# When children are fighting

*I get kind of scared about what will happen with my sister and me. We just keep fighting all the time at the moment, Mum, and you just leave us to it. I think we need help but I don't know how to ask you. You seem so busy and stressed, and last time I asked you just got angry and it was all much worse.*

*Tania comes over to my bed and takes my book.*

*"That's mine!" I say.*

*She throws it on the floor with a smile.*

*That's IT! I have HAD ENOUGH with this!*

*I rush over to Tan, and kind of jump on her. We start to scuffle together, pulling each other's hair. OUCH! That HURTS! I hate this. I don't know what to do. I feel all these feelings and I can see that Tan does too. But I just want to hurt her and she's clearly going for me too.*

*Suddenly, you're in between us, Mum, and you're not angry this time.*

*"Hey lovelies, looks like you need some help! Wanna chase me, instead?"*

*You do that play stuff sometimes, Mum, but it won't cut it this time. I'm too angry. Tan is still trying to get to me, too.*

*"Okay, let's change tack. Wanna tell me what's going on? I'm here to listen to you both. And I'm here to keep everyone safe."*

*We both start talking at the same time. I can hear her saying horrible things about me, so I'm saying them too. We're both shouting. I lunge towards her and try to pull her hair.*

*You move again, Mum, and you hold my hand, and say these weird words:*

*"I'm not willing for you to pull her hair, sweetheart, because I'm here to keep everyone safe, and I'm right here and I'm listening to you both."*

*I try to keep pulling, but you keep hold of my hand and I can't.*

*Tan starts crying. "It hurts!" I hear her say. She cries and cries, and Mum, I hear you tell her that you hear her and you're listening.*

*I start raging. "SHE HURT ME! SHE IS ALWAYS HURTING ME!" I start raging and spitting fire to you, Mum.*

*But you can take it this time, Mum.*

*It's some kind of miracle and I don't know how you're doing it, cos you're stopping me from hurting her and you're listening to me, and you keep turning to Tan and listening to her too.*

*I suddenly feel safe. You've got us both this time. You're going to keep us safe this time.*

*I collapse, and the rage turns to tears. I join in with Tan's crying. We're all sitting on the floor now, and I'm under one arm and she's under your other arm, and you're listening to us both.*

*We both are crying so much. And you stay with us, you keep on staying with us. "I'm here with you both. I love you both. I'm listening to both of you, and I'm going to keep on listening to both of you."*

*Eventually, we both stop, and I glance over at Tan and look in her eyes. I see them glistening with tears. "Sorry, Tan."*

*"I'm sorry too," she replies. We smile at each other, eyes bright, tears drying.*

*"Shall I get a pizza tonight, sweeties, and we can watch a movie together?"*

*"Yes, yes!" we both reply.*

*Phew. That was a really different ending to usual. I'm so glad!*

## About fighting

When children are fighting, it can be so hard for us if we're the only adult present. Being compassionate with ourselves about how hard it can be is so important (especially if it doesn't get resolved like it did in the story).

We have three choices for how to move in: with empathy for each child, mediating between them through talking; with *attachment play* (you can read more about this in the book *Attachment Play* by Aletha Solter, PhD); or with *Loving Limits*. Often we need to experiment to see which is most apt in the moment. Sometimes none of them will go to plan, which is why self-compassion is vital.

# Siblings really do want to love each other, and they need lots of support and lots of listening so they can express all the painful feelings that get in the way of them feeling and being loving.

In order to offer this kind of support to not one, but two children, it is so important to have our own feelings lovingly tended to. This might be through finding someone, or multiple people, who will listen lovingly to our feelings, such as an *empathy buddy*[9], Aware Parenting instructor, or *Marion Method* Mentor, or you might find journaling helpful.

If you want to learn more about mediation, *attachment play*, and *Loving Limits* with children and siblings, I invite you to read *Cooperative and Connected* by Aletha Solter, PhD, and my book, *I'm Here and I'm Listening*.

---

9   This is a term I've borrowed from Nonviolent Communication to describe someone with whom we regularly connect and offer empathy to each other. That might be in person, but it might be via video chat, voice note, or text.

### *Inner Loving Mother* and *Inner Loving Father* phrases

I'm sorry for all the times I didn't support you and your sibling.

I'm here to listen to all the feelings you felt at those times.

I'm sorry for all the times I didn't respond in fair ways.

I'm sorry for all the times I got reactive or angry myself.

I'm here to repair all of those, for as long as it takes.

I'm here to listen to all the feelings.

I'm here to respond in all the ways you really needed.

I'm here to keep you safe.

I'm here to help you when you have feelings in relation to your sibling.

I love you both unconditionally.

I love you both equally.

I'm here to help you both, equally.

CONCLUSION

# Healing is possible

I would never have believed, 37 years ago, that I could become the person I am today. Back then, painful feelings were always flooding out of me, and my inner dialogue was full of guilt, shame, and endless self-judgment. I was identified with my *inner children* a lot of the time.

I didn't know that in becoming a mother, and practicing Aware Parenting, I would experience such deep healing. By offering empathic experiences and expressing loving words to my children, I realised that these same phrases were also what my *inner children* wanted to hear.

> The more I saw how much my daughter and son thrived hearing these statements, the more I offered them to the younger parts of me. And the more those inner children received those words and experienced deep repair, the more I embodied those words as I spoke them to my children.

The whole process became deeply healing. Not only that, but it became part of my calling, as I then began offering these phrases to my mentees, and saw them internalising the words. Many even said that they heard them in my voice. They spoke similar words to their children and then told me that they then heard their children using those phrases to other children and adults.

> You really can have a different inner dialogue.

Your inner children can absolutely heal from past hurts through reparative experiences.

And if you are a parent, that can make a huge difference to your parenting.

*I wonder if you've found yourself in tears reading some of these stories?*

I found myself crying when reading several of them, every time I went through the book.

As Aware Parenting teaches us, we are primed for healing. We innately know how to heal, and we are repeatedly searching for opportunities to do so.

When we cry *while feeling a sense of being loved and held*, deep healing happens.

I'm so willing for you to keep on having beautiful, safe, healing experiences, that support your *inner children* to know that they are deeply loved, and that their feelings are really welcome.

## As we come home to the truth that there was never anything wrong with us, we find that everything in our life changes in beautiful ways.

I'm sending so much love to you and to all the younger parts of you.

Thank you so much for reading this book.


Much love,
Marion


December 2024

## ACKNOWLEDGEMENTS

I really appreciate Aletha Solter, PhD, Founder of Aware Parenting, for her powerful work, her books, her deeply clear thinking, and her wise guidance and support, including editing this book and making editorial suggestions. If you haven't already read her books, I highly recommend reading and re-reading them all. You can find them on her website: **www.awareparenting.com**

I am so grateful to my incredible book publishing consultant, Julie Postance, for yet again helping my book dreams come into form, and to amazing Sophie White, for her beautiful typesetting and cover editing. I absolutely love working with you both!

I love the cover and am sending a big thank you to Jelena Mirkovic for her beautiful creative touch, as always. I loved that we did something a bit different this time!

Editing is always wonderful with my lovely Editor, Belynda Smith. Thank you again, dear Belynda. I love this process of book creating with you.

I really appreciate everyone who was a beta reader, including Joss Goulden, Eirini Anagnostopoulou, Anna Haberfield, Sarah Mason, Irene Perkoulidis, Linde Lambrechts, Kim Cousins, Meg Rankin, and Maru Rojas.

I'm also so grateful to all the parents I have mentored over the years, and who have joined my workshops, groups and online courses. I've learnt so much from you.

Thank you to Michael, the father of my children, for another game of experimenting with lots of different titles before this one emerged!

My deepest gratitude is always to my daughter and son, who taught me the real meaning of inner children and reparenting.

I'm forever thankful to my Dad, and all that he did to support me to follow my dreams.

And to my incredible Mum, thank you for being willing to transform and become my dream mother. You have shown me the power of reparenting, and how we are never too old to heal and grow. Thank you beyond all thank you's for all the times I've asked you to say particular reparative statements to the younger parts of me, and you've done so lovingly and willingly. I love you.

And another big furry thank you to my Frenchie friends, Koyo and Buddha, the most wonderful writing companions.

# GLOSSARY

## Aware Parenting Terminology

*Attachment play*

Nine specific kinds of play between parents and children as described in Aletha Solter's book *Attachment Play*. This type of play creates connection, elicits cooperation, and supports children to both prepare for, and heal from, stressful or traumatic events.

*Balance of attention*

A state in which a child feels physically and emotionally safe while revisiting past stress or trauma. The *balance of attention* is necessary for emotional release and healing to occur (crying, play, laughter, etc.).

*Control pattern*

Repetitive or compulsive behaviours which are usually acquired during infancy and childhood to suppress crying and strong emotions. A typical *control pattern* is thumb-sucking. *Control patterns* can put children into states of mind dissociation. They are also called emotional suppression habits and self-soothing behaviours. They are sometimes called 'repression mechanisms'.

*Dissociation ('freeze or surrender')*

This is one of two primary physiological reactions to real or perceived threats or trauma. (The other is hyperarousal.) During dissociation, the parasympathetic nervous system is dominant, and children are quiet, passive, compliant, inattentive, unresponsive, and numb. They are often using a *control pattern*.

*Emotional release*

Any behaviour which helps restore homeostasis by releasing tension from the nervous system that was acquired during stressful or traumatic experiences. Forms of emotional release in children include crying, raging, trembling, laughter, certain kinds of therapeutic play, and body movements. These are also called healing mechanisms and tension-release processes and are often shortened to the term, 'release.'

### Hyperarousal ('fight or flight')

This is one of two primary physiological responses to real or perceived threats or trauma. (The other is dissociation.) During hyperarousal, the sympathetic nervous system is dominant, and children are agitated, distractible, impulsive, hypervigilant, defiant, reactive, aggressive, or destructive.

### Loving Limits

These are the combination of a verbal or physical limit paired with empathy to create a pretext for a baby or child to cry to release pent-up stress. *Loving Limits* say no to a behaviour or a child's request and yes to the underlying feelings causing the behaviour. (This term was developed by Marion Rose and adopted by Aletha Solter.) We may offer a *Loving Limit* in response to a child's behaviour, such as if they are hitting or biting. We might also offer a *Loving Limit* in response to a child's requests, such as if they are asking us to read them another book and we think they're trying to distract themselves from their feelings. As Aletha Solter says, in this second situation, this is essentially a limit on our own behaviour.

### Suppression

This is when children are disconnecting from their feelings or using a *control pattern* so that they stop feeling their feelings, either when they move their attention to something else, or when we distract their attention away to something else.

## Marion Method Terminology

### Disconnected Domination Culture

The culture that has been firmly in place since industrialisation and has spread around the world through colonisation, but has its roots thousands of years before. The core tenet of disconnection is disconnecting babies from families, and disconnecting us from our bodies, feelings, wisdom, nature, seasons, and traditions. From that disconnection comes domination – force, coercion, guilt, should and have-to, power-over and authoritarianism.

### *Emotional sticks*

These are ways we learn to judge or shame ourselves in The *Disconnected Domination Culture*. Examples of emotional sticks include guilt and shame and all other forms of self-judgement.

### *Healing-feelings*

Feelings that are caused by stress or trauma and when expressed through crying and raging with vigorous movement in loving arms or with loving support, help a child release that stress or trauma and move back into homeostasis. Adults also need to feel safe to be able to express healing-feelings through crying and raging in healing ways or talking to a supportive listener.

### *Needs-feelings*

Feelings that are caused by immediate needs in the present moment and which go away when the need is met.

### *Thoughts-feelings*

Feelings that are created by thoughts. In the DDC, those thoughts can often be harsh, leading to experiences such as guilt and shame.

# RECOMMENDED READING & RESOURCES

### Aletha Solter's Aware Parenting Institute Website

**www.awareparenting.com**

### Books by Aletha Solter, PhD

*Attachment Play: How to solve children's behavior problems with play, laughter and connection*

*Cooperative and Connected: Helping children flourish without punishments or rewards*

*Healing Your Traumatized Child: A parent's guide to children's natural recovery processes*

*Raising Drug-Free Kids: 100 tips for parents*

*Tears and Tantrums: What to do when babies and children cry*

*The Aware Baby*

For more information: **http://www.awareparenting.com/books.htm**

### Books by Marion Rose, PhD

*I'm Here and I'm Listening: Empathic and empowering responses to needs, feelings, and behaviours with Aware Parenting*

*Raising Resilient and Compassionate Children: A parent's guide to understanding behaviour, feelings, and relationships* (Co-authored with Lael Stone)

*Sound Sleep and Secure Attachment with Aware Parenting: Transform sleep for your baby, child, or teen with this compassionate, trauma-informed approach to deep relaxation.*

*The Emotional Life of Babies: Find closeness, presence, and sleep for you and your baby with this compassionate approach to crying*

## Marion Rose's website

www.marionrose.net

## Loving Presence cards by Marion Rose, PhD.

https://marionrose.net/cards

## Aware Parenting Courses by Marion Rose, PhD

https://marionrose.net/aware-parenting-courses/

## Marion Method Courses by Marion Rose, PhD

https://marionrose.net/marion-method-courses/

## Podcasts by Marion Rose, PhD

*The Aware Parenting Podcast*

This was co-hosted with Lael Stone until episode 124.

https://podcasts.apple.com/au/podcast/the-aware-parenting-podcast/id1455772681

*The Aware Parenting and Natural Learning Podcast*

This is co-hosted with Joss Goulden.

https://podcasts.apple.com/au/podcast/the-aware-parenting-and-natural-learning-podcast/id1643837590

*My Marion Method Podcast: The Psychospiritual Podcast*

https://podcasts.apple.com/au/podcast/the-psychospiritual-podcast/id1344385341

## Aware Parenting Community

*The Aware Parenting* (based on the work of Aletha Solter, PhD) Facebook group: This is a free Facebook group facilitated by a team of Aware Parenting instructors.

## WAYS YOU CAN WORK WITH ME

If you enjoyed this book, and would like to work with me, here are some of the ways you can do that.

### Articles on my website
https://marionrose.net/articles/

### Free Aware Parenting Courses
https://marionrose.net/aware-parenting-courses/#free-intro-courses

### Aware Parenting Courses
https://marionrose.net/aware-parenting-courses/#specific-topics

### Aware Parenting Instructor Mentoring Training
https://marionrose.net/aware-parenting-courses/#aware-parenting-instructor-mentoring-course

### Marion Method Courses
(My Inner Loving Presence Process Course is where I show you how you can connect with your Inner Loving Parents and the rest of your Inner Loving Presences.)

https://marionrose.net/marion-method-courses/

### 1:1 Mentoring
https://marionrose.net/mentoring/

## IF YOU ENJOYED THIS BOOK

If you enjoyed this book, I'm so glad! I would love for Aware Parenting and *The Marion Method* to spread to even more people and I wonder if you are willing to consider letting others know about this book as part of that.

Here are some ways you can do so.

Please share your review on Amazon – it helps people see if this book might resonate with them.

Please leave a review on Goodreads.

Are you willing to tell your friends about it via your blog, podcast or YouTube channel, or on Facebook, Instagram, X (formerly known as Twitter), Pinterest or Linkedin?

Are you willing to mention it to your friends and family members or colleagues?

## I so appreciate your support!

ALL OF YOUR FEELINGS ARE WELCOME

## AUTHOR CONTACT PAGE

Email:
**marion@marionrose.net**


Website:
**https://marionrose.net/**


Instagram:
**@_marion_rose_**
**@awareparenting**
**@theawareparentingpodcast**


Facebook:
**https://www.facebook.com/MarionRosePhD**

www.ingramcontent.com/pod-product-compliance
Lightning Source LLC
Chambersburg PA
CBHW020539080526
44583CB00013B/911